First Triathlon:
Your Perfect Plan for Success

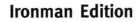

Ironman Edition

First Triathlon:
Your Perfect Plan for Success

Lucy Smith

Meyer & Meyer Sport

IRONMAN® is a registered trademark of World Triathlon Corporation

British Library Cataloguing in Publication Data
A catalogue record for this book is available from the British Library

First Triathlon: Your Perfect Plan for Success
Maidenhead: Meyer & Meyer Sport (UK) Ltd., 2011
ISBN 978-1-84126-116-4

© 2011 by Meyer & Meyer Sport (UK) Ltd.
Auckland, Beirut, Budapest, Cairo, Cape Town, Dubai, Graz, Indianapolis, Maidenhead,
Melbourne, Olten, Singapore, Tehran, Toronto
Member of the World
Sport Publishers' Association (WSPA)
www.w-s-p-a.org
Printed and bound by: B.O.S.S Druck und Medien GmbH, Germany
ISBN 978-1-84126-116-4
E-Mail: info@m-m-sports.com
www.m-m-sports.com

© Dan Smith

CONTENTS

PREFACE:
WELCOME TO YOUR NEW ADVENTURE!

Sometime during the 80's, triathlon started to take off as a sport. Runners and cyclists started learning to swim, swimmers got their land legs and athletes of all abilities discovered that they could start this sport and have fun doing it. Twenty years later, in 2000, Triathlon became a part of the Olympic Games and it was catapulted into mainstream sport culture. Triathlon as a new and modern sport is egalitarian, inclusive of abilities and has a highly professional side.

Where early on, triathletes had to experiment with equipment and training, there are now triathlon clubs for youth and adults, training centres for would-be Olympians, and a plethora of triathlon-specific equipment companies. There is no doubt about it: triathlon is big and it is still a growing sport.

And now you would like to see what this sport is all about. Perhaps you are intrigued by all these fit-looking people training on bikes each weekend, or you are looking for a new goal. Maybe you have seen friends getting into the sport or seen the Hawaii Ironman on television. If you know nothing about triathlon, then this book is for you!

For many years as a youth I was a sailing instructor and taught kids and adults how to get a sailboat from point A to B. For many people, just getting into a small, unstable dingy for the first time was a huge accomplishment. At the end of the session, these same people could sail away from the dock and get back in safely, and could race around buoys. What I remember most from those days was the sense of accomplishment people felt from learning a new skill. I love coaching beginners; I loved being a part of that.

After the sailing days, I became a competitive runner, living my dream of being a full time athlete. Along the way I got injured a few times and during one of these running injuries, I met a triathlete and coach named Lance Watson who showed me the world of cross training and triathlon. I not only had to learn to swim, but I had to learn how to race with people all around me in the water. I had to learn a whole new culture of bikes and equipment and traveling to races. I loved it. As a triathlete I could train more hours outside than I ever could running. I started racing triathlons professionally around the world, earned a degree in education and coaching credentials and married that triathlete who first introduced me to triathlon.

For the last seventeen years, I have been immersed in the sport of triathlon as a coach, athlete and writer. Lance has been my coach for most of that time and I had the amazing good fortune of being able to train at the National Triathlon Centre in Victoria, British Columbia during the time Lance was the head coach there. We had many great Champions and Olympians take part in that group and the coaching excellence that grew out of those years—around the Sydney, Athens and Beijing Olympics and the Hawaii Ironman—had a huge influence on me as a competitor and coach.

All around me the sport was growing in popularity; races were filling up and selling out and local triathlon clubs were increasing in size and number. The sport was booming. Lance Watson and Paul Regensburg started LifeSport coaching, and now we deliver coaching to athletes—from beginner to seasoned professionals—around the world.

And now you would like to start. This is truly a beginner's book. It contains only the fundamental information you will need to do your first triathlon. I have tried to keep it simple and straightforward but to provide enough information to answer the many questions that I know arise from beginners in the sport. My choice to include information has been based largely on my experiences from coaching novice triathletes, from the questions we get at LifeSport clinics and camps and from my knowledge of coaching theory.

The first part of the book contains chapters that cover all the basics, from how to train, how to eat, and what equipment you will need. That is followed by a 16-week Beginner's Training Program geared at completing a sprint distance race. You will want to refer to those early sections while doing the actual training program found in Chapters 9-12. Finally, there is a chapter on reflection and moving forward to bigger goals.

I wish you all the best in this new challenge and journey. I know you will be rewarded well!

Lucy Smith

© LifeSport

CHAPTER 1
Sure Steps to Big Goals

1.1   WHAT IS TRIATHLON?

Triathlon, once a fringe sport practiced by a few hardcore endurance-loving athletes from California and Hawaii, is now one of the fastest growing sports in the world. While three-sport events have been held in Europe since the early 1900's, the first ever modern triathlon was held in San Diego, California, in 1974 and was organized by Jack Johnstone and Don Shanahan. The inaugural event drew 46 participants. In contrast, the now iconic Ironman World Championships in Kona, Hawaii draws 1500 super-fit age group and professional athletes each

year, all of whom have to qualify through prior Ironman performances. Like the Boston Marathon is for runners, Ironman Hawaii is now the dream race for thousands of triathletes. At the 2000 Sydney Olympics, Triathlon made its Olympic debut with 100 men and 100 women participating in respective fields in the Olympic distance event. According to the International Triathlon Union, the governing body of triathlon, no other sport in history has achieved Olympic Programme status quicker.

Triathlon is a challenging, often gruelling, yet relatively safe sport and one that is easy to get into but immensely rewarding for those who stay. It has found its niche amongst a society that relishes personal challenges, growth and fitness. Most people want to complete a triathlon after the first time they watch an event and the number of triathlon events multiplies each year. The exciting and fast-paced Olympic triathlon and the gruelling day-long Hawaii Ironman World Championships have become the cornerstones of the sport and with them have risen athlete personalities, national rivalries, coaching excellence and technical innovations, all of which have made triathlon a mainstream sport.

Triathlon also has something special, and that is that outside the top echelon of athletes looking to make a living from sport, it is a lifestyle sport accessible to a wide range of people. Even with little or no biking or swimming background, athletes can pick up the sport and excel as adults. With the main training emphasis being on fitness and endurance (not on complicated motor skills), anyone with some desire and motivation can start. Triathlon is a sport where you can be as independent as you want or need to be. You will need a pool and a bike, but apart from that, it's like running: you choose where and when you want to train. At races, you will have the camaraderie of hundreds of like-minded people around you. For competitive people who like to set high event goals, there are age group rankings to climb, races to qualify for, age group World Championships opportunities and the thrill of going faster each year.

As the events get longer, so does the extreme sport quotient, with the Ironman presenting a challenge to everyday competitors unsurpassed in many other sports. Ironman typically takes anywhere from 8-17 hours to compete. With its early morning water start, cycling in the midday heat of the sun, and then running home into darkness, Ironman athletes are given emotional, mental and physical stresses that challenges them to overcome and carry on. Nobody is going to hold your hand in ironman; you are responsible for your own hydration, nutrition and physical output for the duration of the event. Ironman is extreme without being perilous or dangerous. Triathlon is a personal test of strength, will and mental fortitude. That challenge has made it a very popular sport for a society that craves real excitement, fitness and personal growth. At the other end, there are the sprint distance races that are over in an hour, but still require athletes to string together three sports as smoothly and quickly as possible.

Triathlon is a multi-sport event encompassing one leg each of swimming, biking and running done consecutively. The swim is generally done in a lake, river or the ocean; although in small community events in the northern part of the Northern Hemisphere, early season triathlons can have a pool swim. Triathlon season usually falls in the Spring, Summer and Fall due to weather conditions, but globally, there are events year-round. Between March and December there are more than two dozen Ironman events worldwide, with eight of those located in North America!

The sport of triathlon has several disciplines: race lengths range from sixty minutes to seventeen hours, and terrain changes with every course. The typical geography of an area dictates the topography and climate of every race, so there are lots of racing possibilities!

The most common triathlon events are:

- **SPRINT:** 750m (0.47 mi) swim, 20km (12.4 mi) bike, and a 5km (3.1 mi) run, and a great distance for a beginner to start.

- **OLYMPIC:** made up of a 1.5km (0.93 mi) swim, 40km (24.8 mi) bike and 10km (6.2 mi) run. This is the only triathlon event in the Olympic Games, but there are World Championships for age groups every year.

- **HALF IRONMAN:** as the name suggests, is half of the venerable Ironman distance: 2km (1.2 mi) swim, 90km (56mi) bike and a 21.1km run. There is a series of events that end in a World Championships each year.

- **IRONMAN**: made up of a 3.8km (2.4 mi) swim, 180km (112 mi) bike and 42.2km (26.2 mi) run. The Ironman World Championship event is held each year in Kona, Hawaii.

Most triathlons start with either a mass swim start or a wave start with tiers of athletes starting at a time, depending on the size of the starting area, but the goal is to race in time trial format (you against the clock) to finish as quickly as possible. (The only exception to this is the ITU professional/elite sprint and Olympic Distance races, where athletes are allowed to draft in traditional cycling packs on the bike). Part of the skill (and fun) involved is learning how to make the transition from swim to bike, and from bike to run, as fast as possible, as that transition time is also part of your overall time that dictates how you do against your competitors. The swim to bike transition is typically called T1, and the bike to run transition is called T2.

1.2   BASIC PLANNING AND PREPARATION

A first-time triathlete ideally will choose a sprint distance race in their home town, or somewhere nearby, for their first race. This distance is a logical starting point and gives a great introduction to the three sport nature of triathlon, and the feeling of racing through transitions for the first time. If you are new to swimming, there can be an opportunity to choose a race with a pool swim. At your first race you will have a chance to meet others in the sport, get a good look at gear that is being used, and possibly be able to ask questions from industry professionals who are set up at the race. Your first race should be simple: about participation and fun and getting to know how it works. As you get more experience in the sport, you can start setting performance goals, using triathlon as a destination sport (places you wanted to see, but didn't have an excuse to get to yet), and to give yourself bigger challenges by racing in hotter climates over hillier course and doing ocean swims.

REGISTRATION

Triathlon is a sport where you will fare better if you are organized about your approach. From choosing a race and signing up, to training and getting equipment, planning and organizing for success is crucial. You will generally have to register and sign up for your first triathlon well in advance of the day. Check with local triathlon shops, recreation centres and online with your regional triathlon organization for a schedule of race listings, and choose a race that is good for you. Keep it simple and stay close to home for your first one if you can. There might even be a beginner's race (often called Try-athlon), or a beginner's clinic offered locally, so do some research. Some races fill up early, so plan ahead and be ready to sign up several months in advance of race day depending on your city. Finding a race about 3-4 months away will give you time to train properly and to gather the correct resources and equipment that you will need.

After registration, at some point, you will be given a packet that will include some, or all of: your race number, information about the race course, the race schedule, the transition zone layout, course rules, and a swim cap. Keep all this stuff safe and read all information carefully. Rules are crucial to triathlon as they keep competitors safe. You can read about triathlon race rules online at your triathlon federation website. Most importantly, take note of when you have to check your bike into the race site, if and when there is a mandatory bike mechanical check and pre-race meeting, and whether there are age group wave starts or one mass start in the swim. We will discuss specific pre-race planning in a later chapter.

1.3   LOGISTICS AND EQUIPMENT

At this point you need to start organizing some equipment. I will go more in depth into equipment in the next chapter, but in order to get started you need to round up a bike and helmet, some running shoes, comfortable, functional running and riding clothing, and a swim suit, cap and goggles.

SWIM:

You will also need to look into your workout environment and start planning where you might do your swimming, biking and running. Check with your local pool for lane swim times, and also for beginner's swim and triathlon clinics, triathlon masters swim programs, or lessons if you need them. Of all the sports, the swim can be the one you have to plan in most as you are restricted by when the pools are open.

BIKE:

Cycling safety should be one of your biggest factors on choosing a place to ride. Many cities now have designated bike routes and bike paths which take bikes away from congested (and potentially dangerous) car traffic, and your goal is to find riding routes that are commonly used by bikes and/or not used that much by cars. Being able to ride without risk of injury from cars, but also uninterrupted by endless traffic lights or cars, is the most enjoyable way to train on the bike. Bike shops and the people who work there are wonderful sources of information for bike routes, many of which are local common knowledge and unmapped.

RUN:

It is often preferable to train on trails to lessen the impact of running and to prevent injury, so research popular running trails in your area. Running on trails is also a nice break from the city streets and sidewalks of your neighbourhood and can provide a strengthening hilly environment, but is not necessary if time constraints make pavement running a necessity. As in riding, finding a running route where you can run uninterrupted by traffic lights and other obstacles is preferable. Local running shops often have a great list of routes for runners, as do clubs.

1.4   ASSESSING YOUR FITNESS AND SKILLS

Are you ready to take on your first triathlon? As long as you are a reasonably fit person, you can organize your exercise time with the goal of completing a triathlon. Triathletes come from many backgrounds. There are many single sport athletes who adapt to the sport: rowers, gymnasts, runners, cyclists, step class experts can all master a triathlon training program. While you may not have done any swimming since grade school, as long as you are comfortable in water and can swim 25 meters straight (preferably front crawl) you can start. You should be able to ride a bike for at least 20 minutes and run for 10 minutes, although using the run/walk method (where you jog for a period, then walk for a period nonstop) is also fine. Individuals without any basic fitness, or who have not been active for a long time, should consult a physician before starting an exercise program. The basic training program in this book is written with the absolute beginner in mind, and will require approximately five hours of your time each week.

The age question: Am I too old to compete in triathlon? The oldest finisher in ironman Hawaii is usually in his eighties. There are no age restrictions in triathlon except in Ironman, where there is a limiter on younger athletes. Triathlons are wonderfully inclusive of all age groups, and as long as an athlete is ready and prepared, age is not a consideration. One of the unique aspects of triathlon, which adds to its popularity, is the fact the athletes of all ages and abilities get to compete side by side with elite and professional entrants.

© Bakke-Svensson/Ironman

1.5 ASSESSING YOUR LIFE SCHEDULE FOR TRAINING

There is a story about making time in our life for the things that matter. The cornerstones of our life are the relationships we have with our family, children, spouse, parents, our education gained, and our health. If you take a vessel and the volume of the vessel is analogous to the finite amount of time you have in a week, you could put in three big rocks to represent these aspects of your life, they take up a lot of space, but all your time wouldn't be spent. If you put sand into the jar next, it will fill in all the spaces between the rocks. The sand represents all the other stuff we do and have, things that are nice but that aren't necessary for our happiness: cars, houses, trips to the mall, reading, parties, watching TV or movies, surfing the internet, doodling, cleaning. There is an amazing amount of room for the sand. However, if you fill the vessel with sand first, the big rocks won't fit: all the small stuff will crowd out the really important things in life. You have time to train; you just have to create it.

Triathlon is a lifestyle sport. Almost all triathletes report that the quality of their life increases when they train for and compete in the sport. Triathlon will make you healthier and stronger both mentally and physically, and if you start to love the sport, as so many do, the training for it will become a part of your life, in varying degrees, for a long time. Making time for your health, for your fitness and for your personal goals has to be something you want to do, you have to value what it brings to your life and you have to be committed to working on it almost every day.

At this point it is good to ask yourself a few questions:

- Can I train for about an hour a day?

- Where will I find that hour a day that I need? Is there flexibility in my life?

- Am I willing to give up some other non essential activities (the 'sand' in the above story) to achieve my goals?

- Have I communicated with those closest to me about my goals?

If you can find answers to these questions then you can start to come up with a schedule that fits your life and your other priorities, such as your small children, or your job. While you will need to train regularly, there is not one set schedule that can work for all people. There might be days, like the weekends, where you have more time to train, or days where you can squeeze in a workout before or after work. Perhaps you have a shower at work and can run at lunch a few times a week instead of walking to the local cafe. Sit down and look at your week and plan which hours will be your training time. Check that pool schedule you found and make note of which pool times coincide with when you have found it possible to train. If you follow the plan in this book, you will need to find about an hour a day, six days a week.

Take note that the information and program in this book is geared at making your foray into a new and exciting sport fun for you. Workouts are geared to be easy to complete and manageable for first time athletes. The overall goal is to teach you something new, and something that can be integrated into your already busy life, but which add value and quality, not something which causes stress. Your mindset from the start should be one of new possibilities: how will I make this work?

Lucy reflects on Time Management:

When I go to triathlons, I watch athletes compete but I frequently see families and I always see smiles. I observe people who work full time sharing triathlon with their partners and children. The first time I watched Hawaii Ironman I marvelled at the groups of fans that some athletes had. I was moved by the passion for life these support groups exhibited. They all appeared to be enjoying themselves and it certainly wasn't a personal sacrifice for them to be there. The fact that Ironman athletes were living out their personal dreams through the most gruelling triathlon that exists, in conjunction with, not in spite of, the rest of their lives was fabulous example of the way your sport and personal life co-exists.

As an athlete you will be tired sometimes. Training, by definition, is about stressing the body repeatedly to make it stronger and more efficient. Not only are you in a perpetual state of fatigue, you are also emotionally and mentally engaged with your racing goals most of the time. Add a partner, kids, and a full time job, and life seems pretty busy. If the attention to all these areas of your life is joyful and positive then you will likely feel energized by your path and by everything you do.

If however, you are doing the reverse—trying to fit your life into a training schedule— there is the possibility that you will feel obsessive and drained by your busy-ness and your personal sense of well being will suffer. Over time, this physical and psychological overload leads to burn-out and dissatisfaction with your life and sport.

Here then are 10 ways to stay energized in your life and sport.

1.   *At the start of the season write down your goals. Write down what you want to achieve, not what you think you should do. This is important to ponder. If your goals do not line up with what you really want, then you will be far less committed than if you embrace your true desire. If you sign up for a certain race because your buddies did, but you really want to test yourself over another course, you won't be as motivated.*

2.   *Once you have your goals written down (and you should write them down) then you need to look at your priorities in life and decide whether your goals match your priorities. If your priorities do not line up with your goals, then you will be frustrated and grumpy about training. It is ultimately more enjoyable to be fully emotionally present at your daughter's Saturday afternoon soccer game than to be worried about the training miles that you aren't getting in.*

3.   *Decide to be flexible and adopt an easy-going attitude about your sport. Plan for your goals to happen by setting short-term goals, a training schedule, or at least a weekly plan that includes time that you can train. At the same time, busy people with demanding jobs and especially parents with small children need to be flexible with their lives. Being able to accept that your children are sick and need you or that you*

have to travel to a business meeting is an easier task if your priorities are clear and you know that over the long haul, you are being consistent with your training.

4.   Be consistent about sleep. Going to sleep and waking up at the same time on a regular basis will ensure you are as rested as you can be. Be aware of the things that will interfere with a good sleep too: alcohol, caffeine and chocolate in the evening, though they may be part of your daily treat schedule, can detract from a good rest.

5.   Understand your energy patterns and organize your day and train accordingly. Most of us have energy highs and lows in the day, parts of the day where we feel most alert and energized and those where we just want to take a nap. If you can, schedule your training around the times when you feel you are at your best, especially if you do only one workout a day.

6.   Go out and play. Participation in sport is playtime: adult fun in a life of responsibility, jobs, mortgages, and other such seriousness. Athletes who have tapped into their inner strength—competing with a sense of happiness and joy—are ones that consistently perform at their best.

7.   Eat well and stay hydrated. Learn as much as you can about good sports nutrition, including what to eat and when, and what proportion of your caloric intake should be protein, carbohydrates and fats. Without being obsessive with your diet, make choices that feed your body and your soul, providing you with adequate energy to support your active lifestyle. Instead of those empty calorie junk foods, replace lost calories with a high nutrition alternative.

8.   Take care of your toys! Be proactive about your equipment and be as organized as you can so that you are always ready to go. There is nothing more aggravating than finding a flat on your bike when you have an hour to ride. Stock up at the bike store with spare tubes and any equipment you may need and keep it on hand by your bike. Have a race equipment list and print it out.

9.   Stretch and strengthen and breathe! Take a Yoga class and reap the many benefits for athletes. Through Yoga you can learn to tap into and increase your core strength, the strength that you need to initiate all other movement in a balanced and efficient way. You will stretch out tired muscles and strengthen and lengthen your back after all the pounding of running. Learning how to really breathe will help in your racing and in your busy life, and most athletes feel rejuvenated and enriched by the mind and body connections of Yoga.

10. Be gentle with yourself. Look at your life and your sport as a work in progress. Each challenging opportunity opens the door for further growth. If your time and energy are limited, make every moment count. On a day that you are tired, give yourself credit for getting out there; savor the sunshine, the forest, the camaraderie of your peers instead of focusing on how slow you feel.

1.6   GOAL SETTING

Having goals, and knowing what it is you want from triathlon is the best way to ensure continued motivation and satisfaction. Staying interested and committed to your training regime takes some planning and a strong sense of where you are going with your season. What are you trying to achieve? There are different types of goals and it helps to be familiar with the various types in order to set goals that are realistic for you.

People train for their own personal reasons. Some want to improve their lifestyle, be more active and feel better about themselves. Some people are satisfying a competitive urge by training for races and trying to win awards and lower personal best times. Not just for Olympians and National Team members, being goal oriented is what fires a lot of people up and keeps them training. Keep in mind that some people are more outcome-oriented (extrinsically motivated by winning, personal best times, weight loss) and some people are more process-oriented (running for an intrinsic sense of well being, to be happy, to feel more efficient as a runner). Knowing what style of athlete you are will help you to set realistic goals for your program.

Dream goals are perhaps the most powerful and personal of the goals: they are the very strong visions you have for yourself. Dream goals set the emotional stage for your passion. Dream goals may never come true, but by acknowledging your dreams you are opening yourself up to vast possibilities that would not exist if you could not let yourself dream these things. Dreams are often private and personal, but also very strong. Dreams about how we see ourselves are the huge positive hopes we hold in our hearts that help us create the sort of life we want to live. The pursuit of dreams is the real path for many people, yet often we ignore our strongest voice out of a fear that others will think us ridiculous or that it may never come true. The path of a dream is a lifelong journey that is worth its weight in gold. To have a dream and to give yourself permission to go for it is what really matters. Dreams are big, and allow us to create short- and long-term specific goals that are in alignment with them. If your dream is to compete in Ironman Hawaii but you've never done a triathlon before, then you have to start with smaller steps. It might take several years of races and training to get there, but your dream keeps you going.

Having a dream goal guides the more specific goals, and ones that you have every ability to achieve today, this week, next month. The more specific and attainable goals that you set are divided into long term and short term goals. Long-term goals tend to be down the road, are bigger goals and are goals that need a longer term plan to achieve, like to complete an Ironman. Long-term goals are important because they make you think about what really motivates you, and what specific things about your dreams you personally would like to accomplish. It is important to identify these long-term goals and to make them realistic and feasible. Your dream goal can be as ambitious as you dare, but your long-term goals should be logical and attainable. Using the Ironman example, your long term goal would be to complete a different Ironman. A long term goal keeps you focused on the big picture as you plan your season, go through the ups and downs of training and racing, and makes planning the short term goals an easier process.

Short-term goals are the stepping stones along the way to the long term goals. These are the daily training sessions you need in order to race your first triathlon, the swimming classes you have to sign up for, and the bike skills you need to improve. They are the things you have to do today, this week, and this month in order to make sure you are moving towards your long-term goals and staying true to your dreams.

Short-term goals can also include races that will create improvement, times that you have to run in training in order to get that personal best and the type and frequency of training that you have to do in order to reach your long term goals. Sometimes short-term goals can look like a to-do list, such as finding a coach to help you build a better training program, buying the proper footwear and signing up for races in advance.

Write down your goals for yourself as they pertain to triathlon. If you don't have huge dream goals, or even a long-term goal, that's quite OK. For a beginner triathlete, it can often look like this:

Goal: to complete my first ever race and to have fun!
Short-term goals: find a triathlon club, clean my bike, organize my training schedule, and finish reading this book so I can get started.

Put your goals on your fridge, on your notice board or anywhere you can see them. Refer to them often, check them off when completed, and look at them on days when you are having a hard time motivating yourself!

CHAPTER 2
Getting Set Up

TRIATHLON EQUIPMENT BASICS

While the possibility to spend money on the sport is limitless, there are only a few basic pieces of equipment you need in order to participate in your first race. In fact, it is advisable to go easy in your first season. With experience, you will learn about what you like and don't like about certain equipment and can make better decisions on purchases. The essential gear for each sport is almost the same gear that is required in the single sport version of swim, bike and run, and most equipment can be bought locally at sports stores, online or through swaps and exchanges. Second hand bikes are economical and easy to get, as are wetsuits, and it's worth looking into used options if you are buying all your gear for the first time.

2.1 THE SWIM

Swimsuit: look for Lycra or polyester racing suits (polyester lasts longer in pools), something that is tight fitting and comfortable.

Goggles: essential for underwater comfort and visibility, goggles come in two basic styles: ones with foam seals for the eye sockets and ones with rubber. Make sure you try both types before buying and get advice on fit and comfort. Goggles should suction to your face briefly without the strap on, and should not dig into your eye sockets. The strap should be set higher on your head, around the biggest part of your skull, not level with your ears, where it is likely to slip down and off.

Swim Cap: keeps hair out of your eyes, out of the pool filter system, and in races, provides visual markers for race officials. Choose a bright one for open water swimming.

Wetsuit: if your race is going to be in cold open water, then a neoprene triathlon wetsuit will be necessary for comfort. Wetsuits are required in most races where the water is colder than 84F. Wetsuits have to fit well, or else they will create more drag in the water (which you really don't need) or hamper your swim stroke. Wetsuit styles can be sleeveless or long-sleeved. Some athletes like the feeling of sleeveless suits better as they allow for more range of motion in the shoulders and don't feel as restrictive around the chest. A long-sleeved wetsuit is ultimately the warmer, more buoyant and more streamlined choice. Just like running shoes, you need to find a good suit that fits well and works in the water for you. A good store will have staff that can help with fit.

2.2 BIKE

Biking is the most technical and gear-dense of the three sports, but in your first season, keep it basic. Beginner triathletes can do a race on a mountain bike or whatever road bike they have in the garage, but 12-18 gears are necessary in order to complete a hilly course or to really change speeds. For your first race, use whatever bike you have or borrow one. If you have a road bike with racing, or drop, handlebars and you find it uncomfortable, go in to a local bike shop and have it fit for you. Adjusting the seat (or saddle) height, changing the saddle, the seat position or the length of the stem (the piece that connects the handlebars to the frame) may be all it takes to gain some comfort. If you are thinking of buying a bike, go to a trusted and recommended retailer and take some time to learn the bikes, and get the right bike for you. Racing bikes for triathlon come in a huge array of frame style, materials and prices: ranging from several hundred dollars to several thousand.

 If you do decide to spend some money on a triathlon bike there are several factors to consider but the two main ones are the frame material and the quality of the components (the moving parts, like gears, gear shifters, brakes, etc.). Frames for racing bikes are either carbon or aluminum, both lightweight and durable, with carbon winning out slightly on the weight end and for comfort. Sets of components (called Groupos) are made by one manufacturer and as such are all one quality. There is a range from entry level to higher end Groupos and it is worth talking to bike specialists about your needs and budget and buying the best Groupo you can afford. Entry level Groupos are generally not recommended for racing, because they are neither durable nor smooth enough to provide the responsive, crisp adjustments needed in racing situations.

2.3 TIME TRIAL VERSUS ROAD BIKE

Triathletes tend to get into this sport and stay for the long haul, and don't mind spending money on equipment that fuels their passion for training and racing, and makes their sport more enjoyable. These days even recreational triathletes who spend three to four days in the saddle each week will have a road bike, a time trial (or TT) bike, and a mountain bike hanging in their bike shed.

The road bike looks like a classic racing bike, like you might see in the Tour de France, with drop handle bars. This bike can be adapted for winter riding easily, with the addition of fenders that keep wet roads from soaking a rider. Triathletes will use the road bike for offseason or winter miles, and when they are doing lots of riding in a pack, where being on the top of the bars with their hands close to the brake levers is crucial for safety. Road bikes are also the style of bike that is used by Olympic distance elite racers as they ride in draft packs and often on very technical courses that require the bike handling of the road frame.

The time trial or TT bike is the most photographed piece of equipment in all of triathlon, and the development of newer, lighter and more aerodynamic racing machines is big business in this world. Any industry magazine has pages of glossy ads, showcasing the latest beautiful, fast racing bikes and the pros who use them. The TT bike is the triathlon racing bike of choice for long distance and non-drafting events. It is equipped with aerobars, which are handlebar extensions that allow the rider to move into a low 'aero' position by resting their forearms on special pads and gripping the ends of the extensions. TT bikes are often made of strong, lightweight carbon, with a very narrow aerodynamic profile that creates as little wind drag as possible. For triathletes racing solo over the Olympic, half and full Ironman distance, having a light, aerodynamic bike saves energy, which turns into a faster bike split, and fresher legs for the run. The seat tube (the tube that runs somewhat vertical below the seat) on the TT bikes is at a steeper angle than a road bike, since the rider is in a forward tilted position while resting on the aerobars.

Whether you buy a time trial or a road bike is up to personal preference and budget. If you can only have one bike, are going to be riding solo most of the time, and see yourself sticking with the sport, racing a lot and have a competitive urge to improve, then the time trial bike might be your best choice. Otherwise, the road bike is a more practical choice, can be adapted for non drafting racing with clip-on bar extensions, and can be ridden year-round and in large groups more safely.

Helmet: Helmets are mandatory race equipment in triathlon and are the best thing to protect your head in case of an accident. Get a helmet and wear it all the time you are on your bike. There are many styles and colors to choose from, but look for one that is safety approved, fits properly, and has some ventilation for hot days. Lighter colored helmets will reflect sun and heat better than dark, a consideration when racing in broad daylight. If you do chance to crash and you crack your helmet, replace it immediately. If a race official notices it during your race, you may be disqualified!

Shoes/pedals: You have two options for attaching your feet to your bike. There are platform pedals, like the ones on the bike you had as a kid, where you just ride in your sneakers on the pedals. You can buy toe clips for these, which are like plastic or metal cages with straps for holding your foot into so it doesn't move around as much. And there are racing pedal/shoe combination pedals, called 'clipless pedals' where you have a plate on your specialized bicycle racing shoe that clips into a specialized pedal receptor on your bike. Clipless systems have been totally adopted in bicycle and triathlon racing for their comfort and efficacy. With your foot clipped to your pedals, there is no extra movement in your lower leg and the power transfer from your body to the bike is as stable as possible. Racing shoes and pedals are definitely the faster, more comfortable option for long rides and racing, and only require a few practice sessions to learn to clip in and out when getting going and coming to a stop. Don't be anxious about trying clipless systems; your foot isn't actually locked in and the action of clipping in and clipping out becomes second nature after just a few weeks.

Glasses and gloves: You will require sport glasses and riding gloves for safety. Never wear metal-rimmed or glass lenses, as these can be dangerous if you fall. Riding gloves are fingerless and padded for comfort, and again, protect your hands in case of a fall.

© fotolia, iceteastock

Shorts: One of the best investments you will make is to buy a proper pair of riding shorts. Cycling shorts are made of stretchy materials and are tight so they don't get caught on parts of your bike or flap around in the wind (slow). They also have a diaper-like (or that's what it feels like the first time you ever put on a pair of riding shorts) padding in them called a 'chamois' that is meant to sit between you and that long, hard, narrow saddle found on racing bikes. That chamois will save your butt. Literally. Once you start riding in training, you will understand. Buy some cycling shorts.

For winter riding, you will also need long tights, waterproof booties that go over your shoes, a waterproof cycling jacket and long-fingered winter riding gloves.

Stationary bike trainer: Not mandatory equipment, but a useful piece if you are not comfortable on the road yet or live in cold, wet climates. A stationary trainer is a strong metal stand that holds your bike by the back wheel, provides resistance on your tire, and allows you to cycle indoors. It is better than an exercise bike as it allows you to ride your own bike and be in a comfortable position.

2.4 THE RUN

RUNNING SHOES

Again, a sport-specific retailer is your best bet for getting the right pair of running shoes for you. All makes of shoes fit a little differently, so trying on various models to find the best one for your feet is important. You will be able to avoid injury with the right pair of shoes, so if you find some that work, buy several pairs to have in store. Once you have your model that works, resist the urge to try different brands or new fads. Stick with what works. You will notice that even major brands of running shoes have cheaper models available at discount retailers. Often these similar looking models are scaled down versions of the technical ones they sell in specialty shops. The higher-end running shoes have superior cushioning, flexibility, responsiveness and workmanship, things you should consider when making your choice. Ask around in your running and triathlon community for referrals and make sure to get fit at a proper running store. Educated employees will be able to check your gait and make sure you are in the right support and cushioning. If you love a pair of shoes, buy two at a time. It saves a trip back to the store, and means you have another good pair in storage for when your shoes wear out.

HOW LONG TO RUN IN A PAIR OF SHOES

This is a hard one to answer definitively because running shoes are so different from each other and each runner is unique in weight, running style, where they train, and just how hard they are on their shoes. Wearing worn-out shoes almost always leads to pain and discomfort in the knees or feet and can lead to other overuse injuries. Because of the durability of the rubber outsoles these days, don't check for wear on the bottom of the shoe, but for the 'dead' feel in the midsole, the blown rubber part that provides cushioning. It becomes unresponsive after a time and also can pack out unevenly. Generally, shoes last about 400 miles. You can do a rough calculation from the time you get your new shoes and mark your calendar for about when that 400-mile mark might be. At that point you can start being aware of a tired shoe and also start looking for another pair, if you liked that one.

RUN APPAREL

For years we all ran in cotton sweats and cotton t-shirts. We were just as fast as we are now, but we are a whole lot more comfortable in our moisture wicking polyester fiber running clothes these days. Your running apparel is the one area where you can branch out and have fun with colors and styles. There is a plethora of excellent running clothing out on the market now, including running skirts and comfortable running bras for women. Get a good running visor or hat: it will make it easier to run on the hot days, protecting your head from the sun.

BAREFOOT RUNNING

No discussion of running would be complete if we didn't discuss the barefoot running debate. It is perhaps one of the most common questions I get asked right now. The barefoot running debate is just that: a debate. There are interesting and educated points of view on both sides, and the debate covers aspects of science, sociology, anthropology, history and evolution. While the discussion and science of biomechanics and foot strength as it relates to running efficiency and health is a good one and worth reading, barefoot running critics point to the fact that running barefoot for training runs is simply not practical for modern, city dwelling athletes who want to train. An athlete can run longer and more comfortably with shoes on simply because she is cushioned and protected from the impact of running and from the hazards on the ground such as rocks and broken glass.

The foot is an amazing piece of engineering and it has its own built-in suspension system, with the arch, and the web of bones that are located there, performing the difficult job of supporting the whole body. Feet that have been in shoes their whole life are not adapted to running barefoot. The foot is also fragile when not strong, so just going out and running barefoot is not advisable without a long and careful progression. Efficient runners and athletes who have strong feet should not have to wear highly cushioned soles with major motion control devices, but comfort should be your first concern.

The debate over barefoot running is interesting, lively and compelling, but it's important to remember that there are no conclusive studies that point to either barefoot running or shod running being better. The only real fact we know is that training is what causes injury. Training too hard, too soon or too long, or a combination of those three is still the only thing we know for sure.

2.5 TRIATHLON RACING GEAR AND OTHER HELPFUL ITEMS

There are some things that have been developed just for the sport to make life easier for competitors:

- **Elastic number belt:** A comfortable lightweight belt that you attach your race number to. It eliminates the need for safety pins and you can attach this to your body after the swim.
- **Water bottle belts:** Meant for longer training runs and competitions, water belts consist of a wide elastic waistband and either one large bottle or 2-4 smaller water bottles so you can carry water distributed evenly around your torso.
- **Hydration systems:** These are fluid carrying bottles with straws that eliminate the need to grasp and hold a water bottle from the frame of your bike. Mounted under the front handlebars, or in the frame, these are popular in long distance races.
- **Chamois butter:** There are creams developed especially for the active cyclist to help assuage discomfort from riding on a saddle. If you find riding persistently uncomfortable to your groin, you can try this out.
- **Racing apparel:** Triathlon suits, or tri suits, are light, tight, bathing suit-like garments that can be worn for all three sports, eliminating the need to change in transitions. They are sleeveless and have long zippers at the front or back for ventilation during the run. Small pockets at the back make it easy to pack along PowerBars and gels. The bottoms can have a small chamois that provides comfort for the ride but is not bulky for the run. One-piece suits are preferred by people who like the comfort of no waistband, but two-piece suits are definitely easier for bathroom pit stops.

© Bakke-Svensson/Ironman

CHAPTER 3
How to Train with Expertise and Confidence

For athletes who have been involved in sport for their whole lives, training sessions become a fundamental part of their path. The early morning swim ritual, the afternoon track practice or the Sunday long run are built in parts of their week and lifestyle. A tennis player or a golfer will spend hours and hours each day in repetitive drills in the effort to be ready to compete. While they have big dreams of races they want to win, or things they wants to accomplish in their sport, the cornerstone of their lives become the daily ritual of preparing to train, executing training and recovering from training.

3.1 DEVELOP GOOD HABITS

Athletes develop habits, both good and bad, around this training. Athletes who bring anxiety to training and who are always trying to prove themselves in workouts are subject to emotional burn out and fatigue. Athletes who fail to warm-up correctly are risking injury while also not giving their bodies a chance to perform optimally. Changing bad habits is time consuming and it takes valuable energy away from training and improving. You have a chance, if you are new to the sport, to develop habits that are positive and that work for you, right from the get go. As you gain experience in the sport, you will learn what works and what doesn't and you will be able to fine tune your training program.

In this chapter we will discuss a positive and logical approach to training and how to create rituals that work for you and take you towards your goal in a productive and joyful manner. Your goal races are future events that keep you motivated towards working hard, your short term goals keep you working in a timely manner towards that big goal, and your training sessions are really the bread and butter, or even the foundation for your whole journey. It makes sense to create a strong, solid foundation: this is your life and health we are dealing with!

3.2 WORKOUT LOGISTICS

- You have a training plan, now look at it! Not just what's coming up today, but what you have planned for the week. It makes sense to look ahead at your schedules, both to plan out your week and to start wrapping your mind around the workouts that are coming up.

- Plan out when and where you are going to complete this workout. Don't leave it up to chance. Know exactly when the workout is scheduled and make sure that you make that time sacred. Know where you are going to train so you aren't making that decision right before the session.

- Choose environments that suit the session to ensure success. A long section of beautiful trail is a far better choice for a long run, than through the city.

- The people you train with are also your environment. Choose training partners that lift your spirits and motivate you, people that are fun to train with and who bring out the best in you.

- Have your gear ready to go and in good shape. Have a designated swim bag that you put a fresh towel in after each workout, or that you leave in your car. Leave your bike ready to ride, not hanging there with a flat tire that you'll "get to later." Keep your riding apparel and gear all in one easy-to-find place in your garage or closet so you aren't scrambling about getting it together before sessions.

- Prepare for how long the session will take. This allows you to plan time for training into your day, around the other tasks you have in your life. I coached one woman who was dreading the long run days because she had a very busy life and would find herself getting anxious about halfway through the run, thinking about all the things she still had to do that day. It was important for her to be able to stay focused on the process of training while she was out there. She figured out a strategy of anticipating the long run and on those days, she would make a list of all the things she needed to do, including the 90-minute base run. Going into the run she would have a concrete reminder that yes, she had time to do the run. This freed up her mind to concentrate on the joy of training and to hold off on obsessing about other details until afterward.

3.3 EXECUTING THE SESSION

For a lot of people, exercising means basically heading out of the door for a required amount of time (or until they fatigue or get bored) then coming home. Training for triathlon requires another level of training, not one that is more difficult, but one that is more effective. Breaking a workout into parts: the warm-up, the main set and the cool down, will allow your body to be more prepared to exercise, and you will be able to maximize what you are able to do on that session. Paying attention to workouts and executing them correctly has tremendous payback: you become a stronger athlete, you learn to stretch your own comfort levels and you are less likely to get injured.

WARM-UP

Before completing a session it is integral to warm up your body well. Warming up is an important step in preparing your body to perform. You need your muscles to be warm and loose and your mind to be focused on giving an effort. A well-warmed up body is ready for the physiological stress of the workout, and a strong mental focus provides the concentration necessary to perform well. A good warm-up therefore is the positive prelude to the great show to come.

A warm-up is nothing more than a period of light, specific physical activity that prepares the body for the activity. It should last 10 to 20 minutes. Give yourself time to warm up and cool down, as rushing through warm-ups may leave you feeling stressed and not ready, and failure to warm-up or cool down well over the long term can leave you at risk of injury. Mentally, use your warm-up to get excited to train but not so nervous or anxious that tension builds in the body. If you feel too nervous about a session, take some deep breaths, relax, and remind yourself of your love of the sport.

SWIM WARM-UP

- Generally, 200-400m of easy swimming and mixed strokes (if you know them) to get going.
- Follow with some lengths of swimming drills to activate the muscles and revisit proper swim form before doing lengths. You can focus on set drills each week, instead of trying to do them all in one session.
- Some athletes need to hop out at this point and stretch their upper body muscles before starting the main set.

BIKE WARM-UP

- Generally speaking, it takes a little longer to warm up for riding than for running because of the greater muscle mass used to cycling and the comparatively lower heart rate when riding easy. Give yourself 15-20 minutes of easy cycling before increasing the intensity and effort on the bike.

RUN WARM-UP

- Stay warm during warm-up. If it's cool outside, leave outer layers on to the extent that you actually feel warm while warming up.
- Jog really easy for 15 minutes, focusing on breathing, being relaxed and having a great posture.
- After a warm-up jog, you can try the run drills described in this book. They will further prepare your muscles for any fast running that is to come.
- Some gentle stretches can follow: glutes, hamstrings, calves and quads. Do not overstretch before workouts.
- For long easy run days, your warm-up can be built right into your run; just head out the door at an easy pace until you feel your natural gait and stride falling into place.
- Cooling down is basically the reverse of the warm-up, a 15-minute very easy jog to allow the muscles to relax and flush some of the waste product accumulated during a session of fast running.

3.4 TRAINING ENERGY SYSTEMS FOR IMPROVEMENT

If you were to follow an intermediate or experience triathlete around for a week, you would notice that she goes at difference speeds in training over the course of the week. One day she will do a two hour ride and be able to talk easily to a training partner, but the next day she will be working so hard on her stationary trainer, that sweat pours off her face and her eyes have the glazed over 'lost in focus' look to them. You might see her at the track running through fast 400m repeats, with very short recovery before she goes again, while the very next day, she is jogging incredibly slow for ninety minutes. At the pool you might observe her swimming a long twenty swim one day and doing a dizzying number of 50's the next at a much faster pace.

This athlete would be following a balanced and prescribed system of training her whole body that addresses her different energy systems. If sitting on the bus for one hour uses your resting aerobic system (you could ride the bus for hours providing there were snacks to fulfill your hunger needs), then sprinting for that said bus when you are terribly late, uses your anaerobic systems (which you can maintain for only about thirty to forty-five seconds). In between these two extremes in rates of effort lie the main energy systems you will use for racing a triathlon, an energy system that you will train to be more efficient, and one that allows you to sustain a certain consistent rate for about an hour.

Put another way, we could take a brief look at pacing as it applies to energy systems and racing. If you have ever watched a kid's running race, at the start of the race they are all enthusiasm and pure joy. Kids take off like race horses out of a gate: arms flying, legs pumping, head back and the biggest grin on their faces because running fast is fun. For them, running is about being a cheetah, about top speed. They are ignorant to the fact that they are using their preciously limited anaerobic system. Fifty meters out of the start, the grins flop to grimaces and their pace slows drastically. Most kids have to stop and walk at this point, because they have been running anaerobically, that is, producing waste product faster than the muscles can clear it away. Walking or jogging slowly forces their body back into the comfortable aerobic state and pretty soon, they are recovered enough to start sprinting happily once more...only to repeat the whole process. No wonder kids like soccer.

Energy is used in your body for all kinds of basic life maintenance like repairing and growing cells and generally keeping you alive. Energy is also used for muscle contractions, whether it is lifting the vacuum cleaner out of the closet or riding your bike up a hill. The rate at which you can work is also a measure of your fitness, which in this book means your cardiovascular strength. If you have ever studied exercise science, physiology or biology you will have studied the three systems that the body uses to produce energy. For those of you who didn't, here is the simple explanation.

THE AEROBIC ENERGY SYSTEM

The aerobic system requires oxygen and this system is used in lower intensity exercise and for the aforementioned body functions. The aerobic system is very efficient and does not produce waste product as the heart and lungs are responsible for carrying oxygen to, and waste away from, the working muscles. Training the aerobic system is the cornerstone of triathlon training. It supports heart and lung (cardiovascular) strength makes your muscles more efficient at using and producing energy and when well conditioned, will allow you to race faster, for longer. To train your aerobic system, you have to exercise for longer than twenty minutes and it has to be at a slow enough rate that you could talk to someone.

ANAEROBIC ALACTIC ENERGY SYSTEM

The anaerobic alactic system is where the body gets its start up energy, and the energy that a world-class sprinter will use to jet down the track. Simply, muscles need a compound called adenosine triphosphate (ATP) in order to contract and fire, but the muscles only store very little of this compound. The body must constantly replenish ATP in order to continue to work. The stores of energy in the muscle that are used up in the intense burst of activity return to normal levels within 2-3 minutes of rest. You will not be spending time developing this system.

ANAEROBIC LACTIC ENERGY SYSTEM

For intense work up to one minute, the body will use the anaerobic lactic system. This system also operates without oxygen, but produces a waste product called 'lactic acid' in the muscles as not enough oxygen is available to remove it. Lactic acid accumulation can most often be felt as a 'burn' in the muscles, to the point where discomfort and fatigue cause the athlete to slow down as a result. The more intense the rate of activity, the faster the accumulation of lactic acid. The body gets rid of lactic acid by switching to a slower rate of exercise and by utilizing the aerobic energy system. It can take up to 2 hours to get lactic acid to return to pre-exercise levels.

NOTE: The first ten minutes of easy, active recovery exercise is the best way to start to 'flush' the legs after lactic build up, one of the reasons why coaches are always getting athletes to cool down right after a session.

Great, so now you know what energy system you use when you have to sprint a block for the bus, but how does it apply to training well? While triathlon is mainly an aerobic sport, there is a range of aerobic intensity that you can perform, from just staying alive to the fine line between staying aerobic (getting rid of waste product) and going anaerobic (accumulating lactic acid because you are working too hard to get rid of waste). Every individual has their own personal "Lactate Threshold" which is the maximal intensity of work that can be sustained using your aerobic system before the body will switch over to the anaerobic lactic system. The higher your Lactate Threshold, the faster you can go for longer. After an athlete has developed a strong level of fitness at the aerobic level, they can start to incorporate speedwork, or more intense work into their training. Working on your lactate threshold (or anaerobic threshold) is what will cause you to improve your pace times from 12min/mile to 8 min/mile.

Speedwork builds the anaerobic threshold (simply, the point at which waste from muscle metabolism overrides oxygen delivery efficiency, commonly felt as the "burn"). Improving threshold performance allows you to race at a faster speed with a lower heart rate, meaning you can go faster for longer than you did before.

Speed training also builds leg strength by creating an ability to hold a longer stride length (which engages more muscle fibers and requires more work) for a greater length of time. Think of it this way: if you take a consistent ninety steps per minute (the average cadence or turnover of trained distance runners no matter how fast they are going), then the only way to go faster is to increase the length of your strides. To increase the length of your strides you need to have strong, supple muscles. Speed work teaches your body to lengthen and strengthen your leg muscles. Athletes who have done speed training can hold dynamic stride and fast cadence for the duration of an event. Because speed training and threshold work are more intense and carry a higher risk of injury, we will only touch on this in the training program, playing with your pace so you can start to learn more than one speed.

3.5   TRAINING BY PERCEIVED EXERTION

While a lot of intermediate programs train by heart rate zones, for the purposes of your first triathlon we will use a system based on rate of perceived exertion or RPE. The program uses RPE training zones as a measure of workout intensity. Please review the table at the end for details of the RPE zones. Zone 0-2 will be mainly aerobic training zones. Your heart rate will naturally rise from sedentary levels, but the rate should feel easy and comfortable. This is the zone that you will do aerobic base runs and recovery runs in. This zone is building your cardiovascular system and providing a strong aerobic platform for your training.

Zone 3-5 take you into higher rates of effort, faster running and more discomfort. Your heart will beat more rapidly, you will need to focus on breathing well and you will have trouble talking while in this zone. (You should not try to talk while in this zone, as it is counterproductive.)

Training by perceived effort is beneficial for beginners to aerobic exercise as it will teach you to listen to your body and it is simple and gadget free. At first, even a slight increase in pace will feel hard and uncomfortable, but over time you will find that your body is adapting to lactate accumulation and you can go faster for longer. The other benefit to training by perceived effort, and not heart rate, is that your body is not a robot. Sleep, stress, coffee, and other environmental factors can affect your heart rate, causing confusion and sometimes stress in athletes trying to obtain unreasonable rates of work. Learning your own effort levels in the absence of a coach is a solid start to training.

On the flip side, to use rate of perceived exertion, you have to be very internally aware and body focused. You have to learn what your paces are, and pay attention to what easy is, and have good judgment about sticking with zones. Athletes who get keen and do too many days in a row at too high rates, will suffer. Eventually their bodies will break down, they will tire and they will not improve. Be honest. Be your own best coach.

3.6 TABLE OF RATE OF PERCEIVED EXERTION

Zone	Pace, Breathing and Perception
0	Rest
1	Very easy pace. Light breathing. Recovery training.
2	Slightly faster pace. Deeper breathing. Conversations are still easy. Base training.
3	Moderate pace. Increased breathing and conversations are getting more difficult. Tempo training.
4	Fast pace. Breathing is getting uncomfortable. Anaerobic threshold training.
5	All-out pace. Breathing is very deep and forceful and efforts feel uncomfortable. Anaerobic capacity training.

3.7 SELF-TALK AND VISUALIZATION

A huge part of doing well in anything revolves around planning for success and seeing yourself being successful at that endeavor. Elite athletes plan for success constantly by taking care of details that affect performance and by using strong visualization to 'see' themselves working at their best and being great.

In every session you should be mindful and alert to what is happening in your brain and in your emotional state. Being tuned into feelings that are calm and confident or their opposite, stress and anxiety, will have great benefit to your overall program. Each time you train you are giving yourself a chance to accomplish something and to be great... and you are ingraining key habits and mindsets that you want to replicate during the more intense race environment. Practice relaxation and the positive mental state that makes training enjoyable and productive (and is the one you need on race day). If you notice negative self-talk about your ability (i.e. "I'm not very good at this") or about sessions that you are dreading, challenge yourself to notice the self-talk, and exchange it for something more positive and helpful (i.e. "I did that session better than last week"). Work on your attitude so that you are reinforcing positive skills. It is proven psychology that mentally preparing for success increases the chances of it being reality. See yourself running, biking or swimming well on those days, executing the skills competently and with confidence.

© Dan Smith

Practice being relaxed for sessions, even when you are tired or not having an 'on' day. Develop ways that you can stay relaxed so as to perform well. This can be rehearsed body awareness cues such as 'relaxed shoulders and back' or ways to calm your mind and refocus on the task at hand. Becoming aware of negative self-talk and training yourself to delete self defeating inner voices is one of the best things you can do for yourself and it will have the added bonus in crossing over and helping in the rest of your life. Remember creating positive habits from the get go is so much easier than trying to change bad habits. Some athletes adopt the practice of journaling and writing down a new mental routine for themselves to affirm a positive behavior until the new behaviors become automatic.

Distractions: One of the most common ways that cause people to underperform is to let themselves get distracted by irrelevant thoughts. Distractions are usually somewhat chaotic conditions that arise unexpectedly and interfere with our perception of how things should be. Triathlon is a sport of distractions: a bunch of strangers are put in the water and asked to swim together, after which they continue to race for anywhere from 1-17 hours in an unpredictable outdoors environment. You have the choice to embrace this 'unpredictable' nature of triathlon and decided to be the best mental athlete out there. The best way to deal with distractions is to refocus on the internal process of what you are doing and decide to get on with whatever really counts. When you are in the flow, distractions slide off your calm and confident exterior.

Reframing is another positive technique in basic sport psychology and includes the ability to transform adversity into a positive. In reframing you take yourself from being a passive victim at the mercy of whatever is happening, to being an active agent in your own course. If you are out there randomly hating the rain, the wind and your bike, you aren't having fun! In reframing, you make an active decision to look at the weather as a challenge to be a better and tougher person. Athletes who can take an advantage out of poor weather conditions, distracting opponents, and fatigue, are athletes that stay relaxed and have taught themselves to 'deal' positively with such conditions.

Working mainly on taking care of the details of planning to complete quality sessions and doing them well is a positive step towards training more effectively. Habits are learned and hard to change, but they can be altered and the more you build positive habits and let go of negative ones, the more powerful an athlete you will be.

© Lance Watson

3.8 TRAINING TO BE GREAT

Training is a path in itself, not just a step towards racing. Training lets us take control of our lives, to do quality work on a daily basis, to create health and strength in our bodies and to build positive habits and routines that make us happy. Training also gets us prepared to execute our larger dream goals. Optimal training requires dedication, planning and a commitment to being our best as much as possible. You have already picked up this book. Within it is an outline for a path you can take to complete your first triathlon. Within you is the energy and passion to make it your own and to accomplish something you are proud of.

Lucy reflects:

So, a good portion of my training energy is devoted to cultivating the kind of mindset that makes me feel good. How do I cultivate this feeling, this confidence? I use my time well. When I am training, I make a commitment to myself to put my best effort into each day, no matter how tired I am, or what has happened in my personal life. I contemplate how I feel when things are going well and the positive thoughts and attitude I have about myself, the world and my training. I work on eliminating negative self-talk, self- defeating behavior and actions that sabotage success.

I like the discipline of training my body and my mind, of practicing how I am going to be confident and joyful on race day. The more I practice being confident in training sessions, the more easily that mind-set surfaces on race day. I like getting to races ready to perform. I expect to be nervous before major competitions as this means that deep down, I care about what I do, but with my well of calm at my centre, the nervousness never becomes debilitating. I work to be free of worry and anxiety, to be able to focus on the process of running well. This practice serves me well, as when I arrive at a big event where the athletic stakes are higher, like a World Championships, I have the comfort of knowing that all the strength and courage I need are right there in my soul.

© Bakke-Svensson/Ironman

CHAPTER 4
Technical Aspects of Swim, Bike and Run

One of the exciting aspects of triathlon is the fact that athletes have to string together three sports in one competition. Often athletes will come at this new sport with familiarity in one or two of the sports and needing to learn the third in order to complete their first triathlon. Learning a new sport, or learning new skills in one sport, like how to corner better on your bike, is one of the aspects that make triathlon so popular and so fun. There are endless ways to learn, to fine-tune expertise and to get better and faster. While this book focuses mainly on the training needed to get you to your first race, it is worth looking at the technical aspects of each sport, as they pertain to triathlon. There are specific drills you can do to become a better swimmer and rider and runner as you gain fitness and confidence in your abilities. Approaching your training with the mindset that you want to be the best you can possibly be right now means that you can always be working on your technique and skill.

4.1 THE UNIQUE CHALLENGES OF OPEN WATER SWIMMING

Swimming in triathlon is more similar to open water long distance than it is to pool competitions. While you might do the bulk of your training in the pool, it is useful to always remind yourself that your races are going to be outside of the comfort of the recreation centre and the lovely black line on the bottom of the pool you can follow as your complete your laps. There will be no wall to turn on and push from nor lane ropes that keep your space wave free and protected from other swimmers.

Swim courses in triathlon vary greatly, from big single-loop rectangles, to smaller square multiple lap courses, to long out and back lines along buoys. Races take place in lakes, water reservoirs, rivers (sometimes with current), and oceans. Swim starts also vary from race to race: there are standing beach starts, waist deep starts, and deep water starts, where you will be treading water before the gun or start signal fires.

One thing is common to all races though, and that is after the start you are going to be in a group of swimmers, sometimes swimming very close to other swimmers, with athletes right behind you, right ahead of you and swimming right beside you as you all race around large buoys for the end of the swim leg. Triathlon swimming is an art form: mastering your best possible swim stroke and speed, while being touched, bumped, and interfered with, and while keeping on course. At the end of the swim leg, you might end up at the beach, at a dock, at stairs or at a ramp, at which point you have to pull yourself upright, and hustle to the transition zone in order to prepare to mount your bike. During this run, you may have to start taking off your wetsuit as well. There's a lot going on!

There are various things you can do in the pool to get yourself ready for triathlon swimming:

Sighting: the practice of looking ahead to where you should be going. Swimming the shortest possible line on the course is your goal, so you have to learn how to take small peeks as you swim, looking for the next buoy (which hopefully is very large and fluorescent orange for visibility).

- Sight by lifting your head slightly before taking a breath.
- Take a small peek before you turn to the side to take a breath.
- Keep your head low to reduce drag between sightings.
- Practice sighting in the pool by using items on deck.
- Practice swimming open water and sighting off landmarks or non-moving objects.
- In a race, look at the buoys and choose landmarks that line up before you start.

Turns: During races you may have to make 4-5 (or more) turns around buoys in your race. This can be another area where the clog of swimmers all funnelling into the turn makes for more body contact.

- As you approach the buoy, either head straight for the turn (the shortest line) or to the outside if there are people and you don't want to be hit.
- Start breathing to one side –the side towards to the buoy– as this will help you sight as you go around.
- Shorten your stroke to get around the buoy, using your close, or inside arm, to drive the body movement around the buoy.
- Sight to the new buoy, then put your head down and lengthen your stroke and get back into rhythm right away.

Fear of open water: For some athletes, getting out into the open water, even if they can swim proficiently, brings up irrational fears and feelings of anxiety. Open water is an unfamiliar environment, unpredictable and often cold, and our vision and breathing are often reduced. The biggest challenge with open water and fear is learning to deal with stress and breathing. As we become anxious and stressed, our breathing become restricted and inefficient. The lack of oxygen creates further stress, especially if you are being splashed in the face from waves or other competitors. Soon, the focus on external environment and the inability to breathe properly creates panic. There are athletes who report thinking of sharks even while swimming in lakes, which indicates the high level of external focus! If you are proficient swimmer, if you have been able to complete the distance in the pool, then you know intuitively that you can complete the open water distance. Learning to swim well outside the pool takes practice and strong internal focus.

- Before jumping in, take some deep breaths and create relaxation and calm in your body. Your first few strokes should be all about the breath and being relaxed.
- Learn to focus on internal cues: breathing, rotation of the body, arm strokes, the kick, your rhythm. Practice deleting non-essential thoughts about the water or your environment. The only environmental thought you need is the direction to the next buoy and avoiding swimmers.
- In races, swim far to the outside of the group to be clear of other swimmers until you are comfortable in groups.
- Practice swimming in open water as much as possible to familiarize yourself with the environment.
- Practice open water swims with another swimmer or group; purposely swim close and with contact and make it fun, not stressful.

- Wear dark goggles on sunny days for better visibility.
- Before races, warm up well, and be ready for your best internal focus.

SWIMMING: FOR ABSOLUTE BEGINNERS

If you are totally new to the sport of swimming lengths, then you should sign up for swim lessons at your local pool, or a learn to swim group with a coach on deck. Learning a few good habits right off the bat will save you time in the swim later on.

4.2 BE THE BEST CYCLIST YOU CAN BE

Your number one priority with cycling is to be safe. Learning road safety and being a safe cyclist should precede learning to go faster. Each year, many triathletes and cyclists are hit by cars while training. Mostly these incidents are the result of human error on the part of the cyclist or the vehicle. Crashes can be devastating, and at the very least can interrupt your training and wreck your bike.

If your experience with riding is tooling around the empty neighbourhood cul de sac on your banana seat bike as a kid, you are going to take that 'riding for fun' attitude, and make it into a race worthy skill! Learning to ride well is something you should value and work on, from cornering, to braking smoothly, to practicing riding safely in groups. Like a car, you need to be in control of your bike. You can go faster, and fall harder on a bike than in your running shoes, but when mastered, riding fast is a thrill like you haven't had since you were eight years old.

© fotolia, benuch

Be a conscious and a conscientious rider, taking pride in your bike skills and good riding habits, and you will be able to train faster, more comfortably and without risk of injury. Basic bike safety:

- Always wear a helmet.
- Follow the rules of the road in your area, and obey stop signs and red lights: you are a vehicle just like the cars you are sharing the road with.
- Avoid emotional confrontations with cars and motorists. These are usually pointless and can sometimes lead to accidents. Instead practice self control, distraction control, reframing and get on with your day.
- Use extreme caution at intersections, looking for cars turning left, and turning right, directly in front of you.

If you are new to a road bike, you can work on drills that will make you more comfortable on the bike. Proficiency on the bike also improves your cycling economy and efficiency, making you a more powerful rider and one who can respond well in race situations. Before doing these exercises, do one basic test. Ride down an empty road on your bike and follow a curb line that is painted on the road. If you can ride straight along that line without wobbling all over the place, you can proceed to the following drills. If your bike wobbles over the road, then practice riding in a straight line until your path irons out. In triathlon, there will be many riders on the course and times when you will be overtaking others, or they will be overtaking you to pass. You need to be able to hold your line and be predictable for the safety of yourself and other competitors.

Tack these onto the end of one of your rides and devote a few moments to mastering your two-wheeled steed. Note: Do these in an empty parking lot or closed road, or a firm grass field.

RIDING WITH ONE HAND

Why? To be able to signal turns, indicate intention to other riders and to be able to eat a gel or drink from a water bottle while riding.

- Start by lifting several fingers off the bars, leaving one hand fully gripping, but relaxed.
- Once you are happy riding with a couple of fingers on the bars, then you can gently lift your hand off the bar, while steering with the other.
- When you're good with this, then you can practice taking your bottle from the cage and drinking from it.
- While all riders have a preferred hand to drink with, practice riding single hand with both hands.

SHOULDER CHECKS

Why? You will need to be able to look behind you to check for cars, and other riders in a race. You always need to shoulder check before making any lateral movement or turn.

- Practice looking behind you, while riding in a straight line.
- Take small checks, shifting your weight subtly on your bike, but not shifting your bike.
- Even though most shoulder checks are to the left, practice to both sides.

BIKE BALANCE AND RIDING CLOSE TO OTHERS:

Why? Triathlon can be crowded, especially right out of transition. Being able to ride close to someone is essential, and if you should touch another bike, this will give you a sense of balance that may prevent a crash. Balance also comes in useful when you need to avoid something quickly.

- On a flat, grassy field, ride side by side with another rider, slowly and at the same speed.
- Ride close enough together that your bodies touch. Lean into each other and continue to ride.
- Do this on a grass field, so that if you topple over, it will be a soft landing. You both need to be riding at the same speed and have to come together and touch hands.

- Ride behind your partner and touch your front wheel gently to her back wheel and feel the change in balance.

CORNERING

Why? There will likely be turns on your triathlon course and riding well through them means both a faster time, and a safer bike. Athletes drifting wide out of turns or braking hard create obstacle for other riders.

- Your inside pedal is up, and you are leaning weight on the outside, down pedal.
- Keep your centre of gravity low to the bike, leaning into your frame.
- Steer the corner wide, angling to the inside of the turn midway, and finishing the turn in your lane again.
- Drop your inside elbow, and apply pressure with the outside hand on the bars.
- Look where you want to go, past the turn.
- Create Figure 8 courses for yourself on empty parking lots and practice!

DESCENDING

Why? There will be hills on some courses, and being able to ride downhill well is an integral and rewarding part of cycling. Descending on a bike is a combination of skills and personality. Some people have the no fear gene a little stronger than others, so the important thing with descending is to always ride within your skill set and experience, while challenging yourself to be better or to embrace the hills.

- Start with short descents that you can do. Find a time of day where there is little traffic, or else a road with a good shoulder to ride.
- Feather your brakes going into the descent, well before the corner so you are at the speed you feel comfortable with before the turn.
- Corner using the above techniques.
- A sure fire way to improve is to follow a better rider down a hill.

CADENCE AND STYLE

Spinning at high cadence promotes good technique and efficient riding—something you want to improve if you are a novice cyclist. "Gear mashing," just muscling through a race in the biggest gear possible, expends a lot of energy and uses up too much precious muscle fuel. Riding is all about finesse. Aim for a high cadence of over 90 revolutions per minute (rpm), and smooth circles – pulling up the stroke as much as pushing down with no dead spots of power at the top or the bottom. You can measure your cadence by counting the rotations of one leg for 30 seconds and doubling it. If you have a bike computer, you can keep track of it this way as well. Keep your upper body still and especially when seated climbing hills. At the moment, you should aim for using a small gear up hills, and climbing while staying seated, being as smooth and efficient up the hill – all your energy making the bike go forwards, not in rocking your body side-to-side or up and down.

A lot of people seem to think that using the small chain ring is wimpy, but being able to ride fast in your small chain ring is the sign of a good rider.

CYCLING: FOR ABSOLUTE BEGINNERS

If riding is new to you, keep it simple. You only need a bike, a helmet and some shoes to ride a bike. Use your running shoes and push on the pedal with the ball of your foot or just behind. Hold the handlebars for balance and control, but relax the "death grip" and stay relaxed in your upper body as you ride to prevent back fatigue. Practice riding in a vacant parking lot or on a bike path in a straight line using the above drills and learn proper road safety before you venture into the city. You don't need specialized gear for your first triathlon; you do need to be in a comfortable position in order to race. You should also take your bike to a shop and have it checked by a mechanic before using it to train, and then again right before your race. It is disappointing to get a flat or a broken cable during a race.

4.3 RUN LIKE THE WIND

If you are coming at triathlon from a running background, then I know what you are thinking: get me through that swim and bike, and let me RUN! The run can be the most challenging and the most gratifying of the legs, partly because running on tired legs is hard, but it's also the leg where you get to run through the finish line: as soon as you are on the run course, all your thoughts start to turn to getting to the end as fast as possible. You only ever get to run off the bike for the first time once. That first time of feeling jelly legs, as you wonder whose body you are in can be quite a shock. Make sure you are proactive at least once, and practice what it feels like to run off the bike!

If you are someone who doesn't feel the joy of running quite the same as those running freaks who seem to glide along, challenge yourself to change your self-talk and your goals, to someone who is learning to 'run fast', instead of berating yourself for being too slow. Find some 5k races to enter so that you can experience running fast and gain some racing experience and confidence.

Run form and biomechanics are topics that are endlessly discussed, and there are many theories and books out there that discuss proper form, footwear, cadence and technique. While reading as much as you can from solid sources is always a good thing, bear in mind that theories about everything come and go in fads and waves. Year round I like to incorporate basic drills into my athletes' programs to keep the right muscles firing and facilitating running energy moving forward with high run cadence. We try to limit eliminating excessive bouncing or side-to-side movement.

For the beginner triathlete, here are some things to keep in mind about proper run form:

* Good posture is essential. Run tall, but not upright, imagining a string pulled out the top of your head, as if you are a marionette. It keeps you tall and long but there is a slight forward lean to your body.
* Be relaxed. A relaxed face and jaw lead to relaxed shoulders and arms and so on down the body. Speed comes from being powerful and relaxed. Tension is slow. Check often for tension and practice being relaxed.
* Keep your chin down and your head still as you tire. Work on keeping posture during fatigue so all your precious energy is moving you forward to your destination.

- Count your steps. Expert runners of all sizes take about 93 steps per minute. This is the most efficient way to run, one where you are using your centre of balance and gravity to run well, and not putting on the brakes with every step. Count one footfall for 30 seconds and double it and this will give you your cadence. Work on getting your cadence into this range. (If you are under 5' or over 6', this cadence will be quicker or slower respectively).
- Practice running off the bike often. Running on tired legs is very different from racing on fresh ones. While you want to do the bulk of your running on fresh legs so as to get very strong, running off the bike will teach your body to adapt to the feelings of fatigue that are unique to triathlon.
- Most triathlon injuries come from running too far too early, not allowing for adequate recovery or from poor footwear. Invest in good shoes and replace then as they wear. Follow a training plan and listen to your body. Pushing through pain almost always results in a regrettable and preventable injury.
- Learn how to stretch and try to make stretching a part of your routine. You don't need to overstretch your muscles, as you aren't looking for the flexibility of a gymnast or a yogi, but taking care of your hamstrings, hip flexors and all the muscles that attach to the pelvis will prevent lower back pain and injuries.

RUN DRILLS

Why? Run drills reinforce proper biomechanics and strengthen the running muscles. This both helps prevent injury, helps you get ready for faster paces in workouts, and delays late race fatigue. A few sets of run drills can be performed after about 15 minutes of warm up running and before the rest of your session.

Run drills should be relaxed and slow, not rushed or tense. The focus is on excellent posture, form and breathing. You do not have to move over the ground very fast, or at all. Start with 10 seconds of each drill and do 2 sets, with a light 2-minute walk or jog between sets. Gradually increase to 20 seconds and 3 sets.

A'S: THE "MARCHING" DRILL:

A's focus on firing your hip flexors (the muscles at the front of the hips) in a rhythmical, dynamic manner. How important are your hip flexors? If you look at a tiny, lightweight Kenyan runner, you will note there is not much present in the way of quad or calf muscles. The best runners in the world are primarily made of lungs and hip flexors. Leg speed and turnover is derived from the hips, and thus the need for working on dynamic strength and muscular endurance in that region. For triathletes running off the bike, often quads are fatigued, and we have to rely on our hip flexor to keep legs moving to maintain run cadence.

- Stand tall and hold your arms relaxed by your side.
- Pull one knee up towards your chest in a firm and deliberate manner. Let drop.
- Pull the other knee up in the same way. Let drop.
- Repeat the 'marching' on the spot for 10 seconds.
- As you improve, swing your arms in rhythm with your marching legs and increase the cadence of your marching.
- You can also bounce a little on the ball of the opposite foot as you pull your knee up.

RUNNING C'S

These are great for heel-lift and building run cadence, and are sometimes called "butt kickers".

A quick, high heel lift contributes to a long fast stride. Again think of the diminutive Kenyan runner running sub-13:00 for 5 kilometers. At that size, the runner is lifting his heel to his rear with every stride, with a very quick rhythm. While this range of motion is overkill for your average runner, an awareness of heel lift and a half-inch more lift can provide you with some extra speed without much cardiovascular cost.

- Stand tall and hold your arms relaxed by your side.
- Run on the spot and attempt to kick your butt with your heels, drawing the heel straight up behind you.
- Land on the ball of your foot and be springy.
- As you improve you can increase cadence.
- Don't move from side to side, but keep everything in a straight line, knees together.

HILLS

Ah! Lovely hills. You either hate them or love them. You see them as a wall or as an opportunity to challenge yourself to be a great runner. Hills will be part of most running routes and triathlons and as such, it's worthwhile developing a good relationship with these land formations and approaching them with a positive mindset. Apart from 'loving' the hills, there are some techniques that will get you up a hill more efficiently.

- Lean into the hill a bit as you start up.
- Use your arms to drive yourself up the hills. 'Strong arms!'
- Increase your cadence up the hill, taking shorter, quicker steps.
- Feel a firm push-off with your back foot.
- Focus on running up and over the crest of the hill.

WATER RUNNING

As an alternative to the pounding and impact of running on land, athletes can take their running into the pool. Called water running, water jogging, or aqua jogging, running in the water is a great way to add mileage to your program without the impact of land running.

Pool running can be an alternative to running on land, or an addition to a regular run training program. Injured, pregnant, or injury-prone athletes can often water run instead of land run, and performing both endurance and quality sessions in the pool helps maintain fitness. When regular run training is resumed, most athletes are able to get back up to speed faster as a result of a water running program.

Pool running is also a useful recovery session to flush tired muscles without the pounding that land running produces. It creates less stress on the body and the gentler environment of water allows athletes to recover faster between sessions.

HOW TO POOL RUN

Run in deep water where your feet do not touch the bottom (a lot of larger pools will have a water running lane in the deep end or dive tank) and until you are proficient with water running technique, wear a narrow flotation belt specifically designed for water running. The belt looks like an 8" strip of high-density foam with a buckle for fastening it tightly to your waist. Many pools have them on hand for aquatics fitness sessions and you may be able to borrow one. With the belt, you can maintain proper body position while focusing on replicating true running form.

Hop in and right away put yourself into a mainly vertical position in the water. Holding your fists as you normally would while running start to pump your arms and allow your legs to follow. Instead of dragging your legs through the water in slow strides, focus on a piston style: drive your knees up and extend your back down to the bottom of the pool. This style will feel more like a drill than your actually running style, but you will be able to maintain a quicker cadence this way. Maintain a relaxed upper body that is vertical with a slight lean forward. Drive the arms as on land and keep the hands closed—do not cup or scull the water. Here are a few additional tips to help you get the most out of a pool-running session:

- You don't have to be concerned about forward speed as much as quick turnover. Driving your legs up and down quickly is the goal.
- Keep hands in a loose fist, as running; do not cup the water.
- Check posture, should be strong from your core muscles.
- Some athletes wear a clean pair of racing or pool shoes to maintain pressure on their feet.

© David McColm

RUNNING: FOR ABSOLUTE BEGINNERS

If you are not comfortable with running for 15', then you can start out with a program that alternates walking and running. A walk/ run program will allow you to gradually adapt to the intensity and impact of running in a controlled way. You should be patient with the progression and build gently into steady running. You can repeat days if you feel you need it, but don't skip ahead. The goal is not to increase intensity but to increase the amount of time spent running so that at the end of the build-up you can run 60 minutes more or less comfortably. The program in this book is a walk/run progression.

RUNNING AND BREATHING

Paying attention to your breath will also help you become a better runner. You should breathe through your mouth and focus equally on the exhalation and inhalation. The exhalation part of your breath is a very important part of your aerobic system and helps the body carry waste products away from muscles and the blood. An efficient exhalation allows your body to get a full gulp of oxygen-rich fresh air to continue the aerobic cycle. Your breathing should be in rhythm with your running to create a smooth and efficient style. Avoid short shallow 'hyperventilating' breaths that create oxygen debt and (sometimes) side stitches.

- While running easy, start to breathe deeply, but relaxed. There should be no tension.
- Notice the relationship of your footsteps to your breathing. How many footsteps do you take between the in breath and the out breath?
- For many people, there is a natural rhythm where the inhalation is always linked to the same side foot strike. (Yours might be different, but work on a regular, relaxed rhythm of steps and breathing.)

THE SIDE STITCH

There is nothing more annoying and mysterious than the 'dreaded' side stitch, that painful stab above your abdomen that comes on in races and makes you want to stop and bend over. There is really no one answer as to why the stitch happens but there is a relationship between breathing and the stitch. The stitch is a cramp in your diaphragm, the large muscle that aids in pushing air in and out of your body. This muscle gets jostled by the action of running as it's also trying to do its work: contracting and expanding. The other organs that reside in and near your rib cage can also affect it, especially your liver, which is why stitches most frequently occur on the right side of the body. All this extra movement can create a spasm in the diaphragm, and pain. Irregular or tense breathing is probably the biggest cause, but there are other factors to consider as well.

TO TRY TO REDUCE THE CHANCE OF STITCHES:

- Don't start runs too fast, especially when out of shape.
- Relax before you start and check often for being relaxed while running.
- Breathe deeply and exhale well.
- Watch your food and fluid intake before running, if stitches are common for you.

IF YOU GET A STITCH:

- Slow down and start to take deep belly breaths and relax.
- Stretch upwards, and to the sides, not by bending over.
- Change your foot strike/breathing combination to exhale on the left foot. This should relieve the pressure caused by striking the ground as the liver falls into the diaphragm.

The side stitch is very common and usually strikes when you are tense or undertrained for the pace you are trying to attempt. Taking note of tensions before running or racing is a good practice at any rate, and may prevent the stitch from slowing you down. If you get a stitch, your attitude becomes your best friend. Instead of dropping into a poor state of mind and feeling discouraged, deal with the stitch in a positive way and get on with your day as best as possible.

4.4 TRANSITION TRAINING

A well-run triathlon includes executing smooth and fast transitions. Also referred to as the 4th leg of triathlon, your transition times are calculated into your overall race time. Practicing smooth transitions will allow your race to be smoother, less stressful and fast. The bulk of triathlon mistakes on race day happen in the transition zone, mainly because athletes are not prepared and have not practiced. You train for hours to improve several minutes over the bike leg, while it only takes 10 minutes a week to practice to shave two minutes off your transition time!

Training for transition includes two aspects: the technical and the physical. The technical aspect includes the setting up of your transition zone, and equipment and knowing what to do when you leave the swim, or come in after the bike. Being able to take off a wetsuit, buckle a helmet, get on your bike or remove shoes quickly and in the heat of competition is purely the result of good drill and practice.

The physical training for transitions involves creating adaptation to the demands of changing muscle and body positions midstream and while doing a high rate of work. Training for the physical demands of transitions are called "brick" workouts: you stack one sport after another. Running for 400m, then hopping on your bike would be a swim-bike brick and running right off the bike, would be a bike to run brick.

TRANSITION DRILLS

(The flow and progression of a great transition is described more fully in the Chapter **"Getting Ready to Race"**.)

- Spend some time practicing T1 and T2 by creating small transition zones at home or at the pool.
- These sessions can be as little as 15 minutes tacked onto the end of your regular training sessions.
- Lay out all your required gear including your bike, run and food, and practice clothing changes and bike mounts and bike dismounts.
- The more you practice transitions, the smoother and more stress-free your event will be and you will exert less effort flailing around in transition. Soon you will find out what gear is necessary for you to bring and how fast you can adapt to the next discipline.

4.5 BIKE-RUN BRICK TRAINING

It is very critical to practice running directly after a bike ride. It is good for you to be aware of the strange sensation you will feel, from "rubber" legs to stiff muscles or just basic tired legs, and to know that after several minutes of running, your body remembers how to run and you will feel more normal and able to complete the run (though likely still tired).

Initially, you will train a walk/jog brick directly after your bike ride. This will ease the transition between the two sports. As your muscles become trained you can decrease your time walking and increase your running time. The first ten minutes is the critical part of the brick workout. Even a short run off the bike, done at regular intervals, leads to muscular adaptation.

NOT JUST FOR THE PROS

While pro triathletes have the distinction of a natural gift for high performance coupled with a single-minded desire to excel and compete, everybody can adopt an attitude of expertise. Taking care of details, leaving no stone unturned and being thorough are part of the can-do attitude of successful people. Be organized and don't overlook important details. Your training plan will be more successful and your race experience will be one that you are proud of!

© Bakke-Svensson/Ironman

CHAPTER 5
Personal Coaching, Online Programs, and Clubs

There are several ways that you can go about starting to train. You can go it alone, using only books, magazines and the Internet as your source of information. You can join a triathlon club and participate in club swim, bike and run workouts, or you can hire your own coach to design a program for you and support you along the way.

The field of coaching and personal coaching has expanded over the last twenty years and there are now qualified professionals and experts who are in the business of providing coaching services to motivated athletes. Having a personal coach used to be the domain of the elite athlete: the coach was a mentor and whip cracker to push them through workouts towards their Olympic dreams. Coaches almost always worked for National Federations at national training centers or for schools and universities. The average age group athlete was left to the resources of her own past sport experience with maybe the bonus of having a volunteer coach standing on deck running a practice.

Coaching is now a viable personal choice in a world where age group athletes are looking for excellence and satisfaction in their sport lives and are willing to pay for the services of a professional who can guide them to their goals.

Coaches are differentiated from personal trainers in that they work with a client on an ongoing basis and have to design yearly training programs that encompass the whole person: the physical preparation, mental well-being, sport psychology and strength training of that individual. On top of the yearly training schedule, coaches are there for offering advice and feedback, guiding career goals and races, creating support and excellent training environments, sticking with you through the lows and highs of your career, and generally being one of the most important support people you will have in your life.

As you can see, from that description there are as many types of coaches as there are personalities of people, and each coach has his or her own strength and weaknesses. Some coaches are better at mental preparation than strength training, and some excel at getting athletes to a peak race. Some of the most respected coaches in the sport of triathlon are natural leaders and guidance counselors, coupled with having a strong background in sport science and triathlon-specific training principles, as well as being people who absolutely love athletes and the sport. A great coach will help you by:

1. Scheduling smart and progressive customized training plans that help you make the most of your time and energy, and that allow you to reach your goals.

2. Offering support in life balancing and sport psychology to help you maximize your potential.

3. Giving technical advice and feedback about equipment, racing and training that supports learning.

© LifeSport

Professional coaches work in a variety of ways, from one-on-one interaction at practices, to delivering training online through e-mail, but the majority of them have a website that outlines who they are, how they coach and what their programs and services cost. Like the individuals that they are, each coach operates in a slightly different way, but here is a breakdown of what you can expect if you do a coaching search:

5.1 ONLINE PROGRAMS

Just as this book contains a training program for you to follow, there are many types of training programs you can purchase off the Internet. The best ones have been created by an experienced and/or certified coach who has designed a schedule that covers any number of months and is geared towards a particular event. You can buy and download the program directly from the Internet site. After that, you are on your own to figure out how to execute the schedule, fit it around your own life schedule, and most importantly, to follow it through. Look for an online program that is designed by a top athlete and/or coach who has experience and certification in the sport. While appealing in price to the first timer looking for some structure, success is limited by individual factors, and lack of interaction with an experienced coach. With generic training programs, you essentially become your own coach so athletes with some background in sport do better here. Knowing what to do and where to find more information when you need it will be an essential part of the process.

5.2 HIRING A PERSONAL COACH

The field of coaching, business coaching and personal coaching is big and growing. Once the bastion for elite athletes who were privileged through genetics to warrant a personal coach, coaching is now accessible for any individual looking for a mentor to assist them in reaching their personal goals. The sport of triathlon is well-suited to coaching because of the intricacy of training for three sports and time management. The typical triathlete is starting in their 30's and 40's and juggling career, family and personal time. They want to get it mostly right the first time, and they want to do well. The understanding of the importance of guidance and leadership has helped create the need for top-level triathlon coaching that is accessible to anyone.

© LifeSport

For a monthly fee, a coach will design a personalized training program for you, will deliver it to you in a timely manner and there will be a method for ongoing interaction between you and the coach, whether it's through a training log online, e-mail, or phone calls. The benefits to this type of coaching situation are that you get a program customized to your life and needs (especially helpful if you are busy person with a full time job and family commitments), and a chance to ask questions. Being able to ask questions and get feedback is one of the best ways to learn in the sport, whether you are a first time triathlete or someone wanting to improve their game. Often these services are tiered and priced accordingly, depending on how much service the individual needs: the frequency and type of interaction with the coach generally dictates the cost of the program. Many coaching programs can also include heart rate feedback, power feedback on the bike, nutritional analysis and guidance, sport psychology, and goal setting. For most folks, this is the most realistic way to hire a coach. It is both more economical than hiring a coach to be with you one-on-one for all your training sessions (like the professional athlete) and it allows you to streamline your training in order to get the most out of each session.

Working with a coach may also give you opportunities to work with them at clinics and training camps. At LifeSport we offer several triathlon camps and clinics each year, where athletes can come for a lively training group environment, personal feedback and analysis and an opportunity to raise their game.

When looking for a personal coach to guide you to your next level in triathlon, it is helpful to understand what you would like in a coach, and what sort of interaction you want to have with this person. You should essentially interview prospective coaches: not only are you going to be paying this person to do a job for you, but you want to enjoy a good rapport that makes your training both fun and productive. Coaching relationships are by nature personal and knowing that your relationship with this individual will improve over time as they get to know you is a good thing to keep in mind as well.

Check their coaching credentials (are they certified through their national coaching federation?) and their background and experience in sport. Coaches who have an extensive background in triathlon, either as coaches or competitors, are good at pinpointing problems and issues and recognizing opportunities for success. Check the coaches' track records and references and compare several programs to find out what sort of service you think you require.

Lucy reflects:

Coaching is not a frill, but an integral part of being an athlete. In my 20-year career, I have always been coached, sometimes by myself. I have learned something from all of my past coaches. I can honestly say that without Lance Watson I wouldn't have achieved the things I did at the height of my career in the last ten years, and probably wouldn't have medaled at two World Championships. Lance has helped me find direction in the sport, choose logical goals and refine my positive mental skills. He has also designed all the major training plans that have led to my being able to race successfully and to my potential at so many important and championship events.

For me, coaching is one of the most important components of being an athlete. What defines coaching right now in triathlon is that through the internet, all athletes can have access to some level of coaching, as opposed to the old model where only elite athletes deserve, or can afford, or can have access to the sort of coaching required to develop to and compete at the top level.

5.3 CLUBS

If you are in triathlon for the social interaction and the lively atmosphere of hanging around with like-minded individuals, then the club option could be your spot. Clubs not only provide triathletes with places to train, set workouts and possibly, coaching, but they are part of your social network. Some cities have a multitude of clubs that now offer training programs and online support to the many triathletes that have joined the sport. For beginners, a triathlon club is like a walking/talking resource on the ins and outs of the sport. Clubs often have inside information on used equipment and can be a great way to pick up your first wetsuit or bike as well. Many clubs now hire a professional coach to design and implement their training schedules, and while each triathlete might be doing more or less volume than the club schedule, training is consistent, progressive and designed around preparing athletes to race. Choosing which club to join is purely a personal preference, but asking around and getting information on what the weekly training looks like, who coaches, and whether the club is more performance-oriented or purely social, is a good place to start.

CHAPTER 6
Getting Ready to Race

A race can be a test of your fitness and readiness and it can be a festival to celebrate the efforts of a lot of dedicated people. Racing is one step more exciting than a training day and gives you a chance to immerse yourself in your sport for a specific period of time. Racing well, like writing exams, is an intense environment that requires strong focus, iron will, impeccable confidence in one's ability and is an opportunity for us to 'raise the bar' on our lives and what we expect from ourselves. Racing generally infuses athletes with a strong sense of well being, as they accomplish goals and push through discomfort and self-defeating beliefs. There is a reason that races are so popular and fill up so fast. People don't seem to just want to train, they want to see what they are made of, and the racing environment provides just that opportunity.

6.1 TAPERING

You have followed the training program, signed up, got your gear and now you are ready to race. Your race day starts about a week before your first event. That last 5-7 days is typically called the taper period, where you reduce the volume and intensity of your training in order to rest and prepare your body for a big effort.

While I have outlined a taper week in the training program, here are some more points to consider.

- Training through the taper week is specific and meant to activate the range of motion for race day. Do short periods of work at race pace.
- You can take a day or two off during the taper, but don't stop completely or you may feel rusty or sluggish on race day.
- Use extra time in your week to check equipment, get your bike looked at and to stretch.
- If you feel antsy during the taper, this is normal. Avoid going for another run, but know that your rest is doing you a favor for race day. A common mantra is that you can't get any fitter in the days before a race, but you can get more tired.
- Continue to eat well, nutritiously and to hydrate.

6.2 ON SITE EXCITEMENT!

If there is an opportunity to pick up your registration and package at the race site a day or two before your event, then you should do this. It really helps to see the environment before the race. Many races will have a technical meeting the day before the race and first time triathletes find the briefing to be very helpful. When you can observe the race site, the transition area, the swim course and even the bike and run course, you will feel more prepared than rolling in blind at 6 a.m. on race morning. Here's what you need to do at the race site before a race:

- Take a look at transition zone, where the bike racks are in relation to the swim exit and the bike and run exits. Note the flow in and out of the transition zone. Note the mount line.
- Go to the swim start and look at the course, noting any landmarks that you might be able to use on race day. If you are allowed into the water, here is an excellent opportunity to practice sighting for the race.

- Ride the bike course if you can, noting hills, corners, technical features. Really take note of course directions; the onus is on you (not the volunteers) to go in the right way on race day.
- Ride or run on the run course, noting the same things as above.
- Take note of where the halfway point is, and one mile to go. Knowing these markers can be incredibly motivating on race day.
- Take a moment to visualize yourself in this environment on race day; see yourself strong and calm and happy. This is your big moment; you want to be able to enjoy it!

Athletes who preview courses report feeling more prepared to race well and less anxious on race morning. Knowing what to expect helps create a more concrete plan about what your race day is going to look like.

6.3 RACE DAY TIPS

On race morning, you are likely going to wake up nervous, and full of anticipation. Do a quick check with your nerves. If you are too keyed up, the tension can play against you, so work on trying to find ways to relax. Merely reminding yourself that you are prepared, and that you deserve to be taking part in this cool new sport is often enough to put the whole thing in perspective. Remember, this is something you are doing to celebrate you, but it's not a major world event, by any means. A few nerves, while annoying to some athletes, mean that you care about the upcoming event and how you will perform. Even seasoned professionals get butterflies on race morning and have to work with strategies to keep that energy positive and not something that will cause them to underperform.

The main thing on race morning is to have a plan and stick with what you always do. Eat the food you are used to and do the warm up you are used to, wear a race outfit or suit you have tested out in training. In other words: Don't change anything from the usual!

- Fuel yourself. About two hours before the event, eat a low-fat, low-fiber breakfast that you have already tested in training sessions. Shoot for a quality carbohydrate that provides a slow to moderate release of glucose, such as old-fashioned oatmeal, cereals that aren't too high in fiber and low-fat yogurt. Toast or bagels with jam is a proven favorite. Also be sure to drink 16 to 24oz of fluid one to two hours prior to exercise to avoid dehydration and aid digestion.

- Be early. Plan to arrive at the race site 60 to 90 minutes before the start. This will allow time for traffic, parking and registration, and give you time to find a spot in transition, set up your bike and run equipment, and memorize flow in and out of the transition zone. This also includes finding the bathroom and changing.
- Warm up. I recommend doing a short run warm-up, especially, if it is a cold morning and a cold water swim. The run warm-up is a great way to raise your heart rate and muscle temperature slightly, and has the benefit of activating the leg muscles which you will use on the bike and run portions of the race. (Running also seems to promote any last minute emptying of bowels and bladder; always a good thing!).
- Do a 10-minute easy jog about 30 to 40 minutes before the start of the race, and follow it with gentle stretching and getting into your wetsuit (if needed). About 15 minutes before the start, jump in the water and do some easy swimming, concentrating on relaxing and practicing sighting to the first buoy.
- Back on the beach, visually locate the course buoys as much as possible as you breath and relax. Look at the first buoy and visualize yourself swimming the first leg and the course. Visualize the start and how it is going to feel. If you start getting nervous: breathe! Breathe and stay relaxed.
- For the last few moments before your start, make sure you are breathing deeply, are relaxed in your upper body and are mentally rehearsing the start of the swim. You are prepared and confident of your ability to compete.
- Pace yourself and enjoy the ride. Athletes who control their thoughts and pace are the ones who feel most successful at the end. Feel happy and proud of yourself while you are racing, noticing how strong you feel swimming, biking and running. Focus only on positive aspects related to your pace, your effort and how you are playing the game!

6.4 SETTING UP TRANSITIONS

While you have practiced transition at home, with your bike up against the house, and in the comfort of your own porch, there are a few more details to note for race day transitions.

- You only have a small spot for your stuff. Only bring into transition what you need for racing. Your bike helmet can be upside down on your handlebars, with your sunglasses perched inside, ready to be put on your face.

- Bike shoes are on the ground in front of your bike (or for more intermediate athletes, already in the pedals), your number belt is beside the shoes, and run shoes are also there, as is a hat for the run.
- You can use a small brightly colored towel on the ground in front of your bike, which acts as a foot wiper and a place marker.
- Put bike in a medium gear, as you will be starting at speed.

A QUICK LOOK AT TRANSITION RULES

- After the bike, you have to rack your bicycle in your spot again.
- You can't interfere with anybody else or their equipment.
- You have to do up your helmet before your touch your bike, and after the bike you have to rack your bike before your undo your helmet buckle.
- You can't get on your bike until the mount line at the entrance of transition
- You can't get off your bike until the mount line.

PROFILE OF AN EXCELLENT RACE TRANSITION (T1):

- Athlete exits the water and immediately pulls goggles to top of head. With free hands, starts to unzip wetsuit and pull it off her torso.
- Runs into transition, pulls off wetsuit as fast as possible and dumps it in a 'neat' pile under or beside bike.
- Takes off goggles and cap and dumps on top of wetsuit, while buckling helmet and placing glasses. Puts on bike shoes and number belt and grabs bike while starting to run out of transition zone with it.
- Mounts bike at mount line and gets up to speed as quick as possible while holding a straight line.

PROFILE OF AN EXCELLENT TRANSITION (T2):

- Athlete approaches mount line and dismounts right before.
- Runs into transition zone with bike and heads to spot to rack bike.
- Takes off helmet, gets out of shoes and puts on running shoes.
- Grabs hat and puts it on while running out of transition zone.

LITTLE TIME SAVERS:

- Vaseline on feet and ankles and wrists can help with wetsuit stripping.
- Elastic laces make it easy to slip shoes on and off. It's amazing how hard it is to tie laces when you are rushed.

- Choose bike shoes with one big Velcro strap, which is easy to tighten.
- Use an elasticized number belt for your race number. You just clip it onto your waist after the swim or the bike.

6.5 HOW TO BE A GREAT RACER

Lucy reflects

"A good portion of my training energy is devoted to cultivating the kind of mindset that makes me feel good. How do I cultivate this feeling, this confidence? I use my time well. When I am training, I make a commitment to myself to put my best effort into each day, no matter how tired I am, or what has happened in my personal life. I contemplate how I feel when things are going well and the positive thoughts and attitude I have about myself, the world and my training. I work on eliminating negative self-talk, self-defeating behavior and actions that sabotage success.

I like the discipline of training my body and my mind, of practicing how I am going to be confident and joyful on race day. The more I practice being confident in training sessions, the more easily that mind-set surfaces on race day. I like getting to races ready to perform. I expect to be nervous before major competitions as this means that deep down, I care about what I do, but with my well of calm at my centre, the nervousness never becomes debilitating. I work to be free of worry and anxiety, to be able to focus on the process of running well. This practice serves me well, as when I arrive at a big event where the athletic stakes are higher, like a world championships, I have the comfort of knowing that all the strength and courage I need are right there in my soul."

Racing is a learned skill: experience will be the best teacher here. The best place to start is to make sure you are racing for the right reasons. While any one event will always have a winner, anybody who finishes is a winner, if they have been racing for the right reasons. Some people race because they are intensely competitive and like to test themselves against peers and even the pros. Racing is all about performance for these people, and that's what drives them. For others, racing is way to test themselves and their training, or a way that they learn to overcome self doubts about their ability. Whatever the reason you are racing, make sure you remind yourself of that on race day. Racing well is a combination of training, personal determination and being aware of the environment, including the people around you.

On race day, you can use hills and corners to be a great athlete. Attempt your best ever performance on the ups and the downs and challenge yourself to be technically good around corners or through rough road. If it rains or is windy, don't let this defeat you or slow you down. Every competitor has to perform under the same circumstances so choose to be focussed and calm.

Think of your competitors as friends, not foes; people that are there to help the race: without them there would be no race and no fun.

Most of all, don't take yourself too seriously. The best performance comes from people who approach the sport with a playful attitude and have decided that no matter what: they are going to have fun!

6.6 VISUALIZATION AND IMAGERY

„If you can imagine it, you can achieve it. If you can dream it, you can become it."
William Arthur Ward

Before the 1976 Summer Olympics, the Soviet Union took pictures of the facilities in Montreal, studied them and pictured themselves competing there. So when they arrived, they had the feeling that they had been there before. Mark Tewksbury went to Barcelona and stood at the aquatic centre and the Olympic Stadium before winning the Gold in 1996. Before Simon Whitfield won the first ever Triathlon Gold Medal in 2000, he trained on the course with his coach Lance Watson. They did hours of training to rehearse exactly the way that Simon would win the medal. While on training camps in Sydney, one of their workouts was running super fast 400m intervals in training because they knew that the race was going to come down to who could finish fastest.

When Simon was running down the final straightaway into first place, he had already run to Gold a thousand times in his mind. In fact, Simon recalls also visualizing how he was going to break the tape, which was by throwing it to the ground in victory.

One of the most powerful tools an athlete can use is that of imagery. Mental rehearsal, imagery, mental imaging and visualization are all terms that describe the exercise of creating a picture of an experience in your own mind. If you have ever been caught daydreaming about a fantastic event you have coming up, or something great happening to you, there is a chance your heart rate was elevated and you feel excited and almost as if it was happening. It is possible to create events in your mind and get the body to physically respond to those events even though they are not really happening.

In the world of high performance, the ability of a person to imagine great things happening, to imagine themselves performing well in a given environment, is often what decides the outcome of the day. For people who have trouble believing that they can do well, using imagery has often created amazing change.

Being able to imagine exactly what you want to have happen on race day increases the chances of those events happening. The trick to imagery and visualization is to be able to clearly see what you want to have happen and the environment where it will take place. One of the reasons it is so good to preview a race course is that when you are visualizing your success there, you can actually see yourself right there on the course!

One of the most commonly used images is one that is meant to visualize your peak performance or your best emotional state, as in the case of the Olympians above. The other is to use imagery to change negative habits into good ones and to create a more positive mind set.

When you are going to visualize your peak performance, you have to be very clear on your goals and what exactly you want to achieve. You can't just skip to the end where you are running through the finish line; you need to see yourself executing goals every step of the way, including your environment, the people there and even the sounds and smells of the event. The more detail you can add, the more real the image is, the more effective the visualization as a tool. If you are visualizing a long event you might have to break your event down into sections and do a little at a time, as you want to see yourself competing in 'real time', not in fast forward.

One other use for imagery is to refocus during an event or workout that is not going the way you expected. If you have generally strong pictures of yourself performing well, executing skills well and being generally positive, you can bring these into play on days where you feel tired or sluggish in warm-up, or just off a little. Instead of being pulled down into a negative emotional state, you can use imagery to buoy yourself. See yourself as a great athlete, as a person who responds positively to adverse situations and you will be able to complete the race or the session to far greater success.

Visualization is a powerful tool, and one that you should start practicing as soon as you start training. Peak performances in sport start in training, in the ability of athletes to imagine their own greatness and success and to work towards this every day.

© fotolia

CHAPTER 7
Fine-tuning Your Program

7.1 SPORT NUTRITION BASICS

What should I eat before a workout? When should I eat before a workout? Should I drink during workouts? Do I need to change my diet before starting my first race? Is beer bad for you? If the field of coaching is booming, then the world of nutrition and particularly sports nutrition has exploded over the last twenty years as more people have become involved in endurance sports and the internet has been able to deliver information that was previously only found in the dusty science journals at the college library. Information that the top athletes in the world have used to improve and maintain fitness and health is now available to anyone with an Internet search engine.

With the growing fitness boom, and our present concerns about our health and longevity, there has also been an increase in the numbers and types of special diets out there, diets that are meant to increase our energy, personal power and stamina. While I don't have the space to critique and review all the current topics in sports and health nutrition, I will cover some of the basics as they pertain to your start in triathlon and how to best approach the training schedule in this book.

7.2 EATING TO FEEL WELL

Still the oldest and most common sense metaphor in the book is the idea of looking at your body as if it is a fine-tuned machine similar to a sports car. The type of gas you use has a direct correlation to how well the engine runs. Looking at food as fuel, the concept is that you want to choose foods that nourish and support your body and the training you desire to do. The reverse to this is training to eat, which is also a driving force for many people: they enjoy food, fine dining and sweets, and training is one way to manage their weight and health. I prefer the eating to live/train version, as it puts the onus on the individual to make healthy, informed choices about what they are putting into their bodies, without being obsessive. Over time, the emphasis on good choices leads to overall feelings of well-being in training and out, and the habits stick for good. Good choices will provide the body with essential vitamins and minerals, and a proper balance of fat, protein and carbohydrates necessary for vitality and health.

CARBOHYDRATES, PROTEIN AND FATS

The three building blocks in food that provide energy to the body are carbohydrates, protein and fats. Carbohydrates are what the body uses most readily for energy. Once eaten, carbohydrates are converted to sugars. Whatever is not needed right away is stored in the muscles as glycogen and used as fuel. Once the glycogen stores are full, the body converts the excess to fat. Because carbohydrates are stored in the body, are converted easily and can be replenished quickly, active people need an adequate supply of carbohydrate to perform exercise. Examples of carbohydrates are bread, fruit, pasta, cookies and crackers. Energy bars for sport, such a Powerbars, have a high percentage of carbohydrates so that athletes can either top up glycogen stores before working out, or can supplement diminishing stores if they are exercising for a long period of time. Once you have run out of glycogen in the muscles, the body has to start converting fat to energy: this process is much slower, so your activity level will be reduced considerably. Called 'hitting the wall', or 'bonking', this is generally an issue for long distance races where replenishing carbohydrates burned is necessary to sustain a high rate of exercise.

Protein is often called the building block of the body for its role in building muscle, hair, bones, skins and other tissue. While athletes don't use a high percentage of protein for workout energy, protein is important for active people as it aids in repairing tissue damage sustained during hard workouts. Protein also has a role in the conversion of carbohydrates to glycogen. For the body to adapt to training, it is constantly repairing and rebuilding: the amino acids in protein are the workers in this process. Active people need about 1-1.5 grams of protein per kg of bodyweight a day.

Fats, while blamed for many health problems in our society, are still an important energy source for the body and help in the conversion of carbohydrates to glycogen. Fat is there to cushion and insulate our internal organs, help with our nervous system and the delivery of some vitamins throughout the body and it is the biggest source of stored energy we have. Fat is a slow to convert energy source that is used primarily when the rate of exercise is low, like walking or hiking or when running an ultra-marathon. It takes the body about six hours to convert fat to energy, which makes it a poor energy choice right before, or during most triathlon events. Most people, even lean ones, have enough stored fat to complete a marathon, so the main concern with fats is to eat the right ones for health.

Saturated fats: mainly from animal sources, saturated fats are solid at room temperature and include butter, cheese and fat in milk, egg yolks and meat. Overconsumption of saturated fats has been shown to be factor in heart disease, obesity and other health issues.

Unsaturated fats are found mainly in plant sources such as nuts and seeds, olives, avocados and fish. These types of fat seem to have a more protective health benefit **and aren't linked to heart disease, so they should be chosen more frequently.**

Trans-fats: these are the so-called 'man made' fats where liquid fats have been converted to solids for the purpose of commercial food production. Most trans-fats are now labeled, because, even if they are vegetable-based (like palm oil) they have been rendered solid and are linked to the same health concerns as saturated fats.

Good choices: There are many resources out there for nutrition and food choice, but nutritionists recommend choosing whole foods as much as you can. Fresh fruit and vegetables, whole grain rice and pastas and bread, eggs, lean unprocessed meat like steak, chicken breast, pork and turkey. Food that is as close to its natural state as possible is the rule to follow. A prepared chicken meal that was prepared three months ago and frozen in a factory is going to be less nutritionally dense than a grilled fresh chicken breast, with fresh steamed broccoli and brown rice. A bagel with almond butter and banana is a better choice than a packaged cookie, muffin or granola bar. Choose lower fat options of foods, and keep fats to a minimum.

Wise choices:
- Fresh fruit rather than a juice, but fresh juice over a sweetened beverage.
- Dark green and colorful vegetables once a day.
- 1% or skim milk rather than homogenized.
- Eat vegetables that are prepared without extra fat, like potatoes rather than French fries.
- Choose whole grain foods and ones that aren't made with a lot of added sugar and fat.
- Select leans meat and prepare without a lot of added fat.
- Choose alternatives to meat often, including fish, beans and tofu.
- Choose sliced turkey and chicken more often than luncheon meats and cold cuts.

Portion: The other aspect to nutrition is serving size or portion: something that North American society has struggled with over the last twenty years. The rise and popularity of fast food, discount shopping and mass consumption has turned bigger into better for everything, including food. Most people eat too large portions for the amount of energy they expend each day, even active people, merely because this is what they are used to. Because of the emphasis on eating more, and eating quickly, people have forgotten how to understand when they are full and to stop eating that point.

Simply put, you only need to eat as many calories as you burn in one day. Eat more than what you use and you gain weight over time: eat less and you gradually lose weight. A healthy person can listen to their body, know when they are hungry, and eat accordingly, stopping when they are full.

Doing exercise is a great way to learn how to eat better. After training, you will often feel hungry, since you might not have eaten for a while and your body is looking for energy to replace the energy it just spent. Making good choices, and fuelling your body slowly and with good quality food until full, will teach you to listen to your hunger signals and to take care of yourself well. How much food you need is very individual and based on a combination of activity level and genetics, and beyond the scope of this book but there are many good quality nutrition books for athletes on the market.

When you eat well, you are setting yourself up to feel well, to improve performance, to help your body repair after exercise and fight illness. The basics to eating for triathlons are to have a general diet that is nutritious, whole, and in line with the energy that you expend each day. For more information on food choices and meals, consult one of the many sports nutrition books available.

7.3   FUELING TO TRAIN

For general triathlon training, there are 3 key aspects to nutrition: 1. Eating and hydrating before workouts, 2. Eating and hydrating during workouts, and 3. Eating and hydrating after workouts. If you have limited time to train, you want to make the most of each session. Being nutritionally ready to perform is very important. For the scope of the training program in this book, and for shorter races of under 90 minutes, hydration and nutrition are not as crucial to success as they are in longer endurance events where athletes will run into depletion during the course of the event, therefore what follows is general good advice that will be a starting point for the beginner triathlete.

Eat before your workouts: You want to start workouts with energy to complete the session, but you don't want to feel full or have stomach upset from something that you ate. Aim to consume 60-100 grams of carbohydrates between 1 and 3 hours before your workout (i.e. half or whole Powerbar and a piece of fruit or a bagel with jam and a piece of fruit). Keep the foods high in carbohydrates and low in protein and fat. Your goal over time is find the right foods and timing that work for you as you will replicate this nutrition on race day. Workout timing has to be taken into consideration. Early morning workouts require only an early breakfast taken prior to training, while evening workouts mean paying attention to nutrition and timing throughout the day. If you train after work (but before supper) you may need to have a pre-training snack (fuel) about an hour before training, especially if lunch was over 4 hours prior. Timing your lunch to fall 3 hours before your afternoon training session is a good practice. You want to avoid skipping breakfast and lunch if you are doing afternoon training sessions. The caloric shortfall of missed meals will leave you depleted and weak in your training. During busy days at work, count backward 1-2 hours from the estimated time you will get to your after work session, and have a snack ready: PowerBar Sport, banana or small sandwich with almond butter and honey.

Hydrate before workouts: It is proven that being dehydrated negatively affects performance. Even a 1% loss in body weight due to dehydration will slow you down, so become friendly with your water bottle! Sipping on water will keep your hydration levels up, but sports drinks, and even juices, contain electrolytes that are more effective at hydrating your body. 1-2 hours before a training session, ensure that you have drunk about 500ml of fluid. Drinking too much too close to a workout doesn't give your body time enough to absorb the fluid. Fluid will either slosh around in your stomach and create cramps and a full feeling, or will hamper you with needing to take bathroom breaks.

Fueling and hydration during workouts: For sessions under sixty minutes, most athletes will only need to sip on water, especially if it is a hot day. The body should have enough glycogen to cover energy demands up to about ninety minutes. For activity over ninety minutes, athletes will need to consume about 200-300 calories per hour for optimal energy to complete the session successfully. A sport gel like PowerBar gel has an easy-to-use pack of 110 calories and a blend of carbohydrates and electrolytes that are scientifically formulated for endurance sports. One gel every 30 minutes of exercise, taken with 8-12 oz of water is recommended and proven to be beneficial to sport performance. There are many gels on the market now, in a variety of flavors. Take the time to find the one that works for you and that you like. Drink 8 oz of water or an electrolyte drink every 15 minutes for the duration of the session.

Every person has a different rate at which they sweat, and there are 2 basic methods of seeing if you are getting enough fluids.

1. The urine test: if your urine is barely yellow, you are well-hydrated. If it is dark yellow, you are not hydrated enough.

2. Weigh yourself before and after exercise. The amount of weight lost is equal to the amount of water lost. For each pound of weight lost, you need to replace it with 20 oz of water.

7.4   HOW TO CARRY LIQUIDS AND GELS

In the pool, you can put your bottle at the end of the lane and sip every 10 minutes or so between lengths. Especially if you are doing another workout in the day, staying hydrated during swimming is important. YES, you do sweat into the pool!

Most bikes come with water bottle cages attached to the frame of the bike. You should be able to store at least one, but preferably two water bottles on your frame. Learning how to reach for and drink from water bottles while moving is a skill that you should practice. There are drinking systems now made for triathlon that consist of a front or frame mounted bottle that has a straw up to the handlebar area for drinking, eliminating the need to reach for a bottle.

Running presents its own problems as carrying a water bottle in your hands is cumbersome and throws you off your natural balance. There are excellent bottle carrying belts on the market now, ones with comfortable wide waistbands that hold several smaller bottles. For long runs over ninety minutes I recommend taking water and gels with you as it will increase your enjoyment and performance of the session.

A lot of running shorts and tights have small pockets build right into them, perfect for carrying along one or two gels.

7.5   EATING POST-WORKOUT

Plan for and aim to eat a small amount of food within fifteen minutes of completing your workout or race. The food you eat should be high in carbohydrates and a similar amount to the number of grams that you should have consumed leading up to the workout. High carbohydrate foods will replace the glycogen your muscles need in order to repair and recover from the stress they were under during your training session. A small amount of protein seems to improve recovery rate as well: half a bagel, low fat yogurt or chocolate milk and a half banana are often a great choice at the post race buffet. Refueling right after a session helps your body recover faster from the session so you are stronger and more ready for the next day. When you are able to train better you will improve faster and will be setting yourself up for success at your race.

7.6 STRETCHING

STRETCHING

For triathletes, stretching refers to the elongation of tissue, which can either be muscle, fascia, or nerve tissues. Stretching either helps us maintain our flexibility or improve it and can be done in a number of ways.

Stretching is a subject with many opinions and views, from how to stretch, to how much to stretch, to whether you need to stretch at all. Coaching advice on stretching will range from never stretching to creating 3-4 one-hour stretching training sessions in your week, each week.

Sports science has shown us that muscles work by stretching. Stretching is the essential action for our muscle. The stretch, and the range of motion (ROM) of each muscle around the bone to which it is attached (the joint) dictates our flexibility. So our flexibility refers basically to how much our muscles can stretch or the range of motion that each muscle has. Flexibility varies immensely from one individual to the next. Even when you were a kid you probably noticed that some of your friends could do the splits, or do back bends, and some couldn't, and everybody notices that flexibility decreases with age. Increasing your flexibility is a way of keeping your body young and supple, and of allowing it to perform better and more pain free.

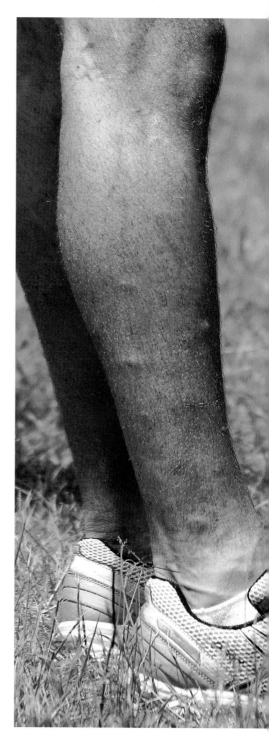

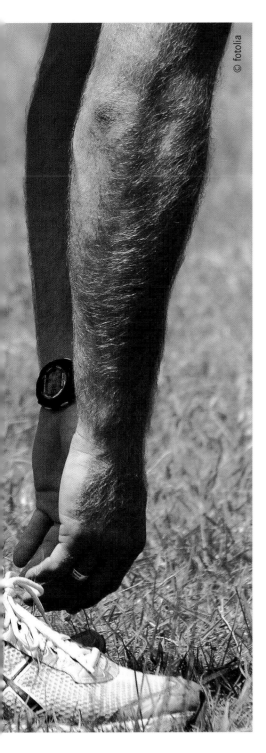

Each individual has an optimal flexibility and range of motion that promotes a healthy, pain-free body. Issues with inflexibility are generally a feeling of tightness in the muscles and joints, pain and injury. Tight muscles do not function to their full range of motion, which means that speed and power are compromised, as will be the natural efficiency for movement. Working on maintaining your body's unique flexibility will allow you to perform better, recover faster from workouts, and reduce the risk of injury.

WE STRETCH TO

- Increase flexibility, and to get the muscles back to their pre-workout length
- Increase performance.
- Improve posture.
- To relax our muscles, which leads to increased blood flow and faster recovery.

HOW TO STRETCH

Stretching will improve muscle flexibility and performance but it is very important not to overstretch, and not to stretch overly tight or cold muscles. Overstretching is counterproductive in athletes, and causes little micro-tears in your muscle tissue that can lead to more soreness and injury.

Some people prefer to stretch before and after workouts, or only before, or only after. Generally it is easier to stretch muscles when they are warmed up a little, after about ten minutes of light exercise. Static (or held) stretches for five to ten seconds are generally the best stretches for returning muscles to their normal state and are most common for triathletes. Holding stretches for longer than two minutes or spending an hour on stretching one muscle group is used for increasing the flexibility of muscles and should be done under the guidance of a professional or by very experienced people. The risk of injury is greater in long stretches and posture and technique are very important. Having poor posture in stretching will usually cause muscles in a different group to be overstretched.

The main muscle groups in triathlon that need to be stretched properly are:

Quadriceps and Hip Flexors: These are the large muscles in your thighs and at your hips, responsible for the dynamic movement of running and cycling.

Gluts, Hamstrings and Periformus: The muscles in your buttocks, hips and the back of your thighs that react to the movement of your front leg muscles contracting. Working on improved flexibility in these areas can help prevent lower back pain associated with running and cycling.

Soleus/Gastrocs (calf): The muscles in your lower legs affect the function of your knees, feet and ankles, which is important to the impact of running and cycling.

Pecs and Deltoids: Muscles in the upper body and torso, help with the elongation needed in swim stroke and strong rotation to get through the water. Because of the postural requirements of stretching, I believe it is highly beneficial to beginner athletes to watch a professional video or hire a professional that can teach them the proper way to stretch and to perform the stretches outlined above. There are good multisport strength and stretching books and videos available. Reading one of these will ensure that you set your stretching program off to a good start.

When and how much you should stretch is going to be something that you learn through experience. The recommendation is to start gently and be conservative, stretching a little before and after workouts. Often, busy people neglect to stretch at all, and rush away from a workout to get back to work. Taking a few extra moments to stretch your muscles post-workout will, like post-recovery nutrition, enable your body to recover faster and better from the session, and set you up for improvement.

CHAPTER 8
Training Plan Overview

Over the next four chapters, you will find your 16-week Plan for your First Triathlon. This schedule is intended for a beginner triathlete with no prior triathlon experience, and has been formulated by LifeSport coaches Lance Watson and Lucy Smith to take you to your first race. The emphasis is on a progression over four months to build endurance and expertise so that you can get to the starting line confident in your preparation and fit enough to complete a sprint distance race. Our goal is to prepare you for success and to make it a fun and enjoyable process. During every session there should be a light-hearted emphasis, even while working hard.

The training program is best executed in combination with all the information and hints throughout the rest of the book, so be sure to cross reference and review often.

The Plan is broken into 4 Phases of 4 weeks each. Each Phase builds on the one before, with overall increases in volume and intensity being built in as the athlete adapts to the training. There will be 'recovery' and 'active rest' weeks also built into the plan. These weeks are important to follow, as they allow the body to adapt to the work, and get stronger for the weeks to follow. Most Mondays are rest days and there is no training. This is to accommodate the longer training that usually takes place on the weekend days. Rest days are good days to still stretch and to plan another alternate activity that you enjoy. As with any training plan, you might have to make adjustments based on your own fitness and comfort level. Instead of adding or subtracting complete sessions or days, try to adjust individual workouts, doing a little less, or a little more. Try to avoid cramming several days together if you miss some sessions. The running is especially spaced to provide as much fitness as possible without the risk for injury. If you are already a proficient runner, then the walk/run program might be too easy for you. You can substitute really easy jogging for all the walking segments. If you feel you want to do more, be conservative. Almost all injuries are a result of overtraining: doing too much, too soon, or too fast. Even professionals continue to make these mistakes late in their careers!

8.1   KEY TRAINING TIPS

Train along a progression from low mileage to high mileage, and from low intensity to high intensity. To really improve, you need the proper phases of training, sometimes over two to three years.

Be patient. Swim comfort, cycling strength and running off the bike take time for the body to adapt to. Consistency and commitment are key. Pay attention to the easy weeks in training. It lets the body adapt to the overload of training and prevents injury and fatigue.

Take care of your head. Use sport psychology to train your mind to be positive and ready for hard workouts and race efforts. Develop an "I can" attitude.

8.2 TRAINING PROGRAM TERMINOLOGY AND EXPLANATIONS

SWIM

D = drill
Fr = freestyle
Br = breaststroke
Bk = backstroke
Kk = kick

Pause 1 drill, also known as Switch 1. Take a stroke and pause on your side while looking at the bottom of the pool. Initiate catch and switch sides. The object is to make the catch strong when you switch to the other side.

Pause 3 Take 3 explosive strokes. On the final stroke, lunge into the side glide position. Glide as far as possible while maintaining good balance. Top arm and hip should be exposed to the air.

Single Arm: With the opposite (non-working arm) at your side. Breathe to the side of the non-working arm. The secret to success with this drill is to complete your breath before stroking. Concentrate on the catch, initiating body rotation with the core body muscles. Take this drill slowly: technique is more important than speed.

Fist: Swim freestyle, but use a closed fist instead of an open palm. Dictates that you have to 'feel' for the water using your forearms, which increases pull efficiency.

Zipper Stroke: Swim freestyle. As the arm recovers, run the thumb up along the side of the torso, pass through and touch the armpit, then continue extending out of the water with fingertips dragging on the surface. This forces full rotation, high elbows, and relaxed hands and forearms.

DPS is Distance per Stroke. Generally a slower stroke rate and you are trying to hold as much water as possible. Concentrate on smooth long stroke with full finish, catching as much water as possible with each stroke. Visualize catching water in your hand and pulling and pushing it like a ball all the way through. Count number of strokes per 25m and mentally make note. Over time, try to swim fewer strokes while maintaining same speed.

BIKE

Single leg: Best done on a stationary trainer or in a controlled environment outside. Unclip one leg from the pedal, resting the unclipped foot out of the way on the frame of the trainer, and pedal with the other leg. You will notice a difference especially on the up stroke and as the foot comes over the top. Try to keep it smooth all the way around without any piston-like actions. You may have to put the bike in a bigger gear for this. You may also become aware of a leg strength imbalance with this drill.

Cd is cadence: How fast you spin your pedals is your cycling cadence. Cadence refers to one complete revolution. Count one leg for 30 seconds and double it, and that is your cycling cadence.

High cadence: Spinning faster than normal cadence (100+) helps build technique and efficiency in cycling. Many beginners typically have a too slow cadence so anything over 90 cd can feel fast.

BG or big gear: Putting your bike into a big (high) gear to create tension builds leg strength and smooth power throughout the pedal stroke. When doing BG, slow cadence to 60-70 and the focus is on tension, not high heart rate or intensity.

Spin: Spinning is the biking equivalent of jogging. It is easy effort, high cadence and oriented to recovery and warming up. (This is differentiated from 'Spin' classes where you use spin technique to elevate the heart rate).

RUN

Strides: Building sprints of 10-20 seconds to build fast twitch, strength, anaerobic alactic system and range of motion.

Brick: A session where you follow one sport with another sport without a break (or stack 2 sessions together like 'bricks'). For instance in a bike-run Brick you will run right after finishing your bike ride, with only a break for changing shoes. A staple workout for experienced triathletes looking to run faster off the bike, and a way for beginners to get ready for the 'jelly legs' of running off the bike. Since biking after swimming is a lot less of an issue than running after biking, most energy is spent in the bike-run brick.

8.3 OTHER PLAN CONSIDERATIONS

PLAN SCHEDULE

The schedule consists of 2-3 workouts per week in each sport. The maximum training volume is around 4 hours per week. There is a complete day off each week on a Monday. Monday has been selected as the day off as experience has shown that it allows an athlete to recover better after a weekend of training. If you already excel in one of the sports

If you have a swimming background and you want to add distance or repetitions to the workouts, you are more than welcome to do that.

If you have a cycling or running background and feel the need to add volume to the program, you are welcome to do that as well. Work within the volume you have already established, understanding that you are putting in several more hours of cross training each week.

IF YOU NEED IMPROVEMENT IN ONE OR MORE OF THE SPORTS

On the opposite extreme, if you feel as though you need help in one area or the other, you may want to drop a workout that you are strong in, and add an extra where you need improvement. If you feel the need to add a swim lesson in place of a swim workout on the schedule, by all means take the swim lesson and don't feel the need to make up the missed swim workout.

WALK/RUN SCHEDULE:

This plan is built around a walk/run schedule that is meant for beginners who have not been doing much running. The walk sections are important for maintaining an aerobic effort of RPE 1-2, and to reduce the risk of injury. All the running throughout the 16 week schedule is built around the walk/run training method as I feel it is the least risky way to present a run schedule in a book for beginners, a schedule that is built for your success. On race day, you might want to test yourself to jog the whole run leg, or use a combination or walk and run, which I outline in the chapter: Getting Ready to Race.

BIKE

The majority of the bike workouts are in RPE 1-2. However as the plan progresses, there is a little more work in RPE 3. The longest ride in this program is 1 hour. In the last block of training you will be practicing running off the bike on your Sunday ride. This is called a Brick on the schedule.

RUN

As with the bike workouts, the majority of your running will be in RPE 1-2. If you need to walk to stay in that training zone, that is ok. As you get fitter then you will find it easier to stay in the zone. In the later weeks of the program, there is an opportunity to run at a higher intensity (RPE 3) in order or you to play around with the pace of your running and effort levels. Keeping this in mind, if you run on a hilly course frequently, you might find that in the first few weeks you have to walk more than the program requires in order to keep your effort really aerobic and easy.

The aim of this program is to allow you to train for a triathlon with the least possible disruption to your life. Look through each week and decide early in the week when and where you will fit your training in. Make plans in advance, schedule your training time and let yourself look forward to these sessions. The goal is to integrate training into your life and allow your training and competition to enhance your life rather than become an added stress in your already busy life.

© Bakke-Svensson/Ironman

CHAPTER 9
Your 16-week Training Guide: Weeks 1-4

The first phase is meant to get you going. You will start to build your general fitness and commitment to a program. Your comfort level in the swim, on the bike and on the run should increase during these weeks. Copy the training into a calendar and preview each week on Sunday. Focus on building skill and paying attention during sessions. Completing sessions well and with a positive mindset is your goal.

9.1 WEEK 1

Total training time: 2hrs 15min
All workouts aerobic, RPE 1-2

Monday: OFF

Tuesday: Swim 20 minutes
100 meters (m) warm-up (choice stroke)
8 x 25 m freestyle (fr) (15 seconds rest)
4 x 50 m (as 25 backstroke/25 freestyle with 15 seconds rest)
100 kick (kk) with kickboard
100m cool down choice

Total: 700m

Wednesday: Run/walk 20 minutes
5 min warm-up walking
4 x (1 min jog/ 2 min walk)
3 min cool down walk

Thursday: Bike 20 minutes, flat loop
10 min warm-up spin
5 min high cadence focus on spinning smoothly with 85-90 cd
5 min cool down spin
**If you do not have an odometer on your bike to show you your cadence, then, every few minutes, count how many times one leg rotates in 15 sec then multiply this by 4 to receive your cadence reading.*

Friday: Swim 25 minutes
100 m warm-up choice
10 x 25 m fr
2 x 50 m (15 seconds rest) (as 25 breaststroke/25 freestyle)
3 x 50m (15 seconds rest) (as 25 backstroke/25 freestyle)
150m kk (with kickboard)
100m cool down choice

Total: 850m

Saturday: Run/walk 20 minutes
5 min warm-up walking
3 x (2 min jog/1 min walk)
2 x 30 sec faster than jogging pace with 1:30 min recovery walk between efforts
2 min cool down walk

Sunday: Bike 30 minutes
10 min warm-up spin
5 min as 10 seconds standing/ 50 seconds sitting recovery (put bike in 2 gears harder for standing)
5 min high cadence (spin 85-90)
5 minutes cool down easy spin

9.2 WEEK 2

Total training time: 2hrs 30min
All sessions RPE 1, 2 with some 3 where indicated

Moving into week 2, the emphasis is still on building your fitness and increasing comfort and skill in the three sports. You should research a timely race at this point, and start collecting gear that you may need. You should be starting to gain a feel for your fitness and effort levels at this point.

Note: This week rest or recovery intervals are indicated like this: (20"). (" means 'seconds' recovery; ' means 'minutes')

Monday: OFF

Tuesday: Swim 25 minutes
200m warm-up, choice stroke
6 x 25 m freestyle (with 15 seconds rest) concentrate on faster arms every 2nd 25m.
5 x 50 m (15 seconds rest) as 25 breaststroke/25 freestyle
10 x 25m (15 seconds rest) kk (as 1 easy, 1 effort)
100m easy cool down, choice stroke

Total: 950m
**Faster arms means speed up your swim stroke, turning over your arms faster in the water.

Wednesday: Run/walk 20 minutes
5 minute warm-up walking
4 x (1:30 min jog/1:30 min walk)
5 minute warm-down walk

Thursday: Bike 25 minutes
5 minute warm-up spin
5 min as high cadence focus on spinning smoothly with 90 cd
5 min as alternate 30 seconds harder gear (RPE 3) and 30 seconds easy gear recovery
10 minute cool down spin
**For the harder gear, you should feel some tension in your legs to push a higher gear, but pedalling should be smooth.

Friday: Swim 20 minutes
100 m warm-up choice
6 x 25m freestyle as (1 free/1 drill, with 15 seconds rest) Drill: Finger tip drag
4 x 50 m (25 seconds rest) fr as 25 fast arms/25 recovery
2 x 50m (20") as 25 breaststroke/25 freestyle
100m choice kick (grab a kickboard)
100m cool down, choice stroke

Total: 750m
**Fingertip drag: slow your freestyle stroke down a bit and concentrate on dragging your fingertips across the top of the water alongside your body during the recovery phase of the stroke (when your arm is above the water). Also called Zipper because the action is like pulling a zipper up from your thigh to your armpit. This focuses on maintaining a relaxed arm and a high elbow.

Saturday: Run/walk 20 minutes
5 minute warm-up walking
3 x (2 minute jog, 1 minute walk)
4 x (15 seconds faster than jogging pace **(RPE 3)**, 45 seconds recovery walk)
2 minute cool down walk

Sunday: Bike 40 minutes
15 minute warm-up spin
5 min as 10 seconds standing/ 50 seconds sitting recovery (put bike in 2 gears harder for standing)
12 min as 2 min high cadence (spin 90-95) 1 min easy
8 min cool down easy spin

9.3 WEEK 3

Total training time: 2hrs 55min
All sessions RPE 1-2 this week.

Welcome to the third week of the training plan. At this point you should be learning that you have more than one speed but the sessions are manageable and smooth. Stretching should not be ignored as for some people the new muscles being used are creating soreness.

Note: This week rest or recovery intervals are indicated like this: (20"). (" means 'seconds' recovery; ' means 'minutes')

Monday: OFF

Tuesday: Swim 25 minutes
200m warm-up, choice stroke
8 x 25 m (20") freestyle
3 x 50 m (20") as 25 backstroke/25 breaststroke
8 x 25m (20") kk (all at easy effort, working on kicking with relaxed feet)
6 x 25m (20") freestyle (easy, working on distance per stroke-DPS)
100m easy cool down, choice of stroke

Total: 1000m
**Distance per stroke: *working on lengthening out your stroke by rotating on your side and reaching as far forward above the water as possible before entry, and feeling water through the whole stroke to a long and complete finish. There should be no pause. Take a stroke count for each 25m and try to decrease your stokes-per-length throughout the set and schedule.*

Wednesday: Run/walk 25 minutes
5 minute warm-up walking
5 x (2 minute jog, 1 minute walk)
5 minute cool down walk

Thursday: Bike 30 minutes
10 minutes warm-up spin
5 minutes as high cadence spin at 95.
3 x (30 seconds harder gear/tension/ 30 seconds recovery spin). Stay seated.
10 minutes cool down spin

Friday: Swim 25 minutes
100 m warm-up choice
8 x 25m (15") freestyle (as 1 fr, 1 drill) Drill: Pause 1
4 x 50m (DPS or distance per stroke, with 30 seconds rest)
200 kick easy
100 m cool down, choice stroke

Total: 1000m
**Pause 1 drill, also known as Switch 1. Take a stroke and pause on your side while looking at the bottom of the pool. The object is to make the catch strong when you switch to the other side.

Saturday: Run/walk 25 minutes
5 minutes warm-up walking
4 x (2 minute jog, 2 minute walk)
5 minute cool down walk

Sunday: Bike 45 minutes
15 minutes warm-up spin
2 x 10 minutes (5') high cadence 95+
10 minutes cool down spin

9.4 WEEK 4

Total training time: 3hr 10min
All sessions RPE 1-2, with 3 indicated

You are now ready to complete your first month of training. If you have been consistent, you are already stronger and fitter than when we started and able to handle some more intensity in training. This week I will challenge you to get your heart rate up a bit on some sessions. Starting next week there is the opportunity to do sessions on a stationary bike trainer. See if you can borrow, or buy one before next week.

Monday: OFF

Tuesday: Swim 25 minutes
200m warm-up, choice stroke
8 x25 m (20") fr (as 1 fast arm, 1 recovery swim)
4 x 50m (20") (as 25 backstroke/25 freestyle)
4 x 50m (25") fr (working on DPS)
6 x 25m (20") kick with board (as 1 fast RPE 3/1 easy)
100m easy cool down, choice of stroke

Total: 1050m
During DPS see if you can reduce number of strokes per 25m over last week.

Wednesday: Run/walk 25 minutes
5 min warm-up walking
2 x (2 minute jog, 1 minute walk)
4 x (30 seconds jog, 30 seconds slightly faster than jog pace RPE 2-3, 1 minute recovery walk)
5 minute cool down walk

Thursday: Bike 35 minutes
10 minute warm-up spin
5 minutes cadence 95
5 x 1 min as 30 seconds higher gear/tension RPE 3/30 seconds recovery spin)
Keep cadence 90+
15 minute cool down spin

Friday: Swim 25 minutes
100m warm-up choice
10 x 25m (20") freestyle drill (as 1 glide to 3, 1 fingertip drag)
6 x 50m (30") DPS (distance per stroke)
6 x 25m (20") kicks freestyle (as 1 easy, 1 fast)
200 m cool down, choice stroke

Total: 1000m

Saturday: Run/walk 30 minutes
10 minute warm-up walking
3 x (2 minute jog, 1 minute walk)
3 x (15 seconds jog, 45 seconds faster than jog pace RPE 2-3, 1 minute recovery walk)
5 minute cool down walk

Sunday: Bike 50 minutes
15 minute warm-up spin
4 x 2 min (1') high cadence spinning (95+) flat course
4 x 30 (1') seconds standing (put in 2 gears harder for standing)
5 minutes faster biking RPE 3 and cd 90
10 minutes cool down spin

9.5 DID YOU KNOW?

Exercise makes your heart stronger, helping it pump more blood with each heartbeat. The blood then delivers more oxygen to your body, which helps it function more efficiently. Exercise can also lower blood pressure, reduce your risk of heart disease and reduce levels of bad cholesterol, which clogs the arteries and can cause a heart attack. At the same time, exercise can raise levels of good cholesterol, which helps protect against heart disease.

CHAPTER 10
Your 16-week Training Guide: Weeks 5-8

After a month of training, you are ready to take it up a notch. This month will see a slight increase in mileage and intensity, but the focus is still on endurance and skill. There will be some rides that can be done on a stationary trainer, if you have one. Develop and maintain good eating and resting habits to ensure your body and immune system stay strong.

10.1 WEEK 5

Total Training time: 3hr 30min
All sessions RPE 1-2, with 3 indicated

Monday: OFF

Tuesday: Swim 30 minutes
100m warm-up, choice stroke
8 x 25m (15") freestyle (as 1 fast arm, 1 recovery)
4 x 100m (45") (as 50 backstroke/50 freestyle)
4 x 50m (20") freestyle (DPS) *don't rush this*
200 easy cool down, choice of stroke
Total: 1100m

Wednesday: Run/walk 30 minutes
10 minute warm-up walking
4 x (30 seconds jog, 30 seconds faster than jog pace RPE 3, 1 minute recovery walk)
3 x (2 minute jog, 1 minute walk)
5 min cool down walk
**This week, you want to feel the pace change for faster than jog pace. Remember to stay relaxed and maintain form and technique while increasing your intensity.

Thursday: Bike 35 minutes (stationary, if you have one)
10-minute warm-up spin
4 x (25 seconds left leg spinning, 35 seconds both, 25 seconds right, 35 seconds both)
2-minute recovery spin
4 x (30 seconds high cadence spinning (95+), 30 seconds recovery)
10 minute cool down spin
**If you are riding on a stationary trainer, you can do single leg riding with the resting foot off the pedal. Outside, it is more practical and safe to just focus on one leg and let one leg be relaxed.

Friday: Swim 25 minutes
100m warm-up choice
10 x 25m (20") (as 1 freestyle, 1 backstroke)
6 x 50m (30") (breathe every 3)
3 x 50m (20") kick (as 25m easy, 25m fast)
200m cool down, choice stroke

Total: 1000m
****Breathe every 3: only take a breath every third stroke, working on rotating well in the water.*

Saturday: Run/walk 35 minutes
10 minute warm-up walking
3 x (2:30 minute jog, 1:30 minute walk)
2 x (30 seconds jog, 30 seconds faster than jog pace RPE 3, 2 minutes recovery walk)
5 minute cool down walk

Sunday: Bike 55 minutes
15-minute warm-up spin
4 x (30 seconds left leg focus, 30 seconds recovery spin, 30sec right leg focus, 30 seconds recovery spin)
5 x (30 seconds standing, 1:30 seconds recovery spin) *Put bike in 2-3 gears harder for standing efforts*
2-minute recovery spin
4 x (30 seconds hard gear- low cadence 65-70, 1:30 min recovery) *Put bike in hard gear and feel tension on full pedal stroke.*
10 minutes cool down spin

Next week we will be keeping the session lengths the same, but adding just a dash more intensity. The goal here is to not rush through anything, to take things in stride and to listen to your body.

10.2 WEEK 6

Total Training time: 3hr 50min
All sessions RPE 1-2, with 3 indicated

This week sees an addition in some intensity. As always pay attention to your nutrition – making sure you are getting an adequate amount of proteins, fats and carbohydrates, along with minerals and vitamins. This will help your fitness levels, aid in recovery and provide you with enough energy stores to last through the gradually longer distances.

Monday: OFF

Tuesday: Swim 30 minutes
200m warm-up, choice stroke
6 x 25m (15") freestyle (as 2 fast arms, 1 recovery)
2 x 150m (45") (as 50m freestyle/50m backstroke/50m freestyle)
4 x 50m (20") kick (as 25m fast, 25m easy)
200 easy cool down, choice of stroke

Total: 1050m
**When working on kick, concentrate on loose feet, kicking from your core and kicking up with your feet, as well as down.

Wednesday: Run/walk 30 minutes
5 minute warm-up walking
2 x (3 minute jog, 1 minute walk)
4 x (1 minute jog, 30 seconds faster than jog pace RPE 3, 1 minute recovery walk)
5 minute cool down walk
**When running fast, feel all your energy propelling you forward. Keep upper body relaxed.

Thursday: Bike 40 minutes (stationary)
15-minute warm-up spin
3 x (30 seconds high cadence spinning (95+), 30 seconds recovery spin)
2-minute recovery spin
5 x (25 seconds left leg spinning, 35 seconds both, 25 seconds right, 35 seconds both)
10 minute cool down spin
**Single leg work: as the interval increases in length and your leg becomes fatigued, remember to maintain foot rotation and consistency throughout the entire pedal stroke.

Friday: Swim 30 minutes
100 m warm up choice
6 x 25m (20") (as 1 freestyle, 1 backstroke)
8 x 25m (30") (as 1 breath every 3, 1 breath every 5)
6 x 50m (20") kicks freestyle (25m easy, 25m fast)
200 m cool down, choice stroke

Total: 1000m
**Breathe 3 or 5: only take a breath every third or fifth stroke. Remember that breath control is essential when it comes to swimming. You don't hold your breath while running or riding your bicycle, so why would you while you are swimming? When holding your breath for up to five strokes, remember to release the oxygen by blowing out at a steady pace – don't hold your breath until the last stroke, likewise don't breathe all of your air out on the first stroke.

Saturday: Run/walk 40 minutes
10 minute warm-up walking
2 x (3 minute jog, 2 minute walk)
3 x (15 seconds jog, 45 seconds faster than jog pace RPE 3, 3 minute recovery walk)
10 minute cool down walk

Sunday: Bike 60 minutes
15 minute warm-up spin
4 x (30 seconds left leg, 30 seconds recovery spin, 30 seconds right leg, 30 seconds recovery spin)
3 minutes recovery spin
2 x (45 seconds standing RPE 3, 1:15 seconds recovery spin) *Put in 2-3 gears harder for standing efforts.*
3 minute recovery spin
4 x (30 seconds big gear- low cadence 65, 1:30 minute recovery spin)
15 minutes cool down spin

10.3 WEEK 7

Total Training time: 2hr 50min
All sessions RPE 1-2, with 3 indicated

This seventh week has a noticeable decrease in overall mileage and time. This is an active recovery week. You are still training and touching on some different energy systems and while making sure that your heart rate is getting up, however, the mileage is backed off to give you a physical and mental break from the training load. While you might feel energized and want to train harder, be patient and let your body rest and adapt.

Monday: OFF

Tuesday: Swim 20 minutes
100m warm-up, choice stroke
4 x 50m (15") freestyle (as 2 fast arms, 2 recovery swim)
3 x 100m (45") (as 50m DPS/50 kick with a board)
100m easy cool down, choice of stroke

Total: 700m
**When working on kick, concentrate on loose feet, kicking from your core and kicking up with your feet, as well as down.*

Wednesday: Run/walk 25 minutes
5 minute warm-up walking
1 x (3 minute jog, 1 minute walk)
3 x (1 minute jog, 45 seconds faster than jog pace RPE 3, 2:15 minute recovery walk)
5 minute cool down walk
**When running fast, think of having quick feet across the ground.*

Thursday: Bike 35 minutes (Stationary)
15 minute warm-up spin
3 x (15 seconds high cadence spinning 100+, 45 seconds recovery spin)
2 minute recovery spin
2 x (25 seconds left leg spinning, 35 seconds both, 25 seconds right, 35 seconds both)
10 minute cool down spin
***Single leg work: as the interval increases in length and your leg becomes fatigued, remember to maintain foot rotation and consistency throughout the entire pedal stroke.*

Friday: Swim 20 minutes
200m warm-up choice
6 x 25m (15") freestyle (DPS)
6 x 50m (20") kicks freestyle (25m easy, 25m fast)
200m cool down, choice stroke

Total: 700m
***During DPS see if you can reduce number of strokes per 25m.*

Saturday: Run/walk 30 minutes
5 minute warm-up walking
4 x (2 minute jog, 2 minute walk)
2 x (30 seconds jog, 30 seconds faster than jog pace RPE 3, 2 minute recovery walk)
10 min cool down walk

Sunday: Bike 40 minute
15 minute warm-up spin
4 x (30 seconds left leg, 30 seconds both, 30 seconds right leg, 30 seconds both)
10' as riding with focus on cadence 90.
10 minutes cool down spin

10.4 WEEK 8

Total Training Time: 4hr
All sessions RPE 1-2, with 3 indicated

At the end of this week, you will be at the halfway mark of the training plan. That's GREAT! You can give yourself a pat of the back and know that you have the mettle to take on your first triathlon. This week is the last phase of training to build your base endurance. You should feel rested after the active recovery from last week. With the highest training volume yet, make sure you are eating well, stretching and getting enough sleep.

Monday: OFF

Tuesday: Swim 30 minutes
200m warm-up, choice stroke
4 x 50m (15") kick (as 25m easy, 25m fast RPE 3)
5 x 75m (30") freestyle (as 25m breath 3, 25m breath 5, 25m breath 3,)
6 x 25m (20") freestyle (as blast first 15m, easy to the end)
100 easy cool down, choice of stroke
**Freestyle blast you are turning arms over quickly and working hard (RPE 3-4) for 15m.*

Total: 1000m

Wednesday: Run/walk 30 minutes
5 minute warm-up walking
3 x (30 seconds jog, 30 seconds faster than jog pace RPE 3, 2 minute recovery walk)
3 x (3 minute jog, 1 minute walk)
5 minute cool down walk
**Faster than jog pace: see previous week(s) on triathletemag.com.*

Thursday: Bike 40 minutes (stationary)
15 minute warm-up spin
4 x (30 seconds left leg spinning, 30 seconds both, 30 seconds right, 30 seconds both)
3 minute recovery
3 x (30 seconds high cadence spinning (95+), 30 seconds recovery spin)
10 minute cool down spin

Friday: Swim 30 minutes
200m warm-up choice
4 x 25m (15") freestyle (DPS)
4 x 100m (30") (as 75m freestyle/25m double arm backstroke)
6 x 25m (15") freestyle (as 15m blast, easy to end)
200m cool down, choice stroke

Total: 1050m
**Double arm backstroke: both arms pull and recover at the same time. This aids in loosening up and relaxing the shoulders.*

Saturday: Run/walk 40 minutes
10 minute warm-up walking
2 x (3 minute jog, 2 minute walk)
2 x (30 seconds jog, 45 seconds faster than jog pace RPE 3, 2:15 minute recovery walk)
10 minute cool down walk

Sunday: Bike 60 minutes
15 minute warm-up spin
4 x (30 seconds left leg, 30 seconds both, 30 seconds right leg, 30 seconds both)
3 minute recovery spin
6 x (45 seconds standing, 2:15 seconds recovery spin)
15 minutes cool down spin
**When standing: Make sure that you aren't leaning on your handlebars. When you lean your weight onto your arms, you lose quite a bit of leg force, and your legs are what will propel you forward out on the road! You should concentrate on driving your foot down the centre of your pedal with one leg, and pulling up with the other. Rock your bike, not your body as you pedal.*

Starting next week, I will be incorporating a bit of heart-rate work and adding in some flippers and swim pull-buoys to the next training block. If your local pool doesn't have the equipment, look at investing in some. If not, simply do the work without these training devices.

10.5 DID YOU KNOW?

Proper breathing is an underestimated, but critical building block of good health. Slow, deep breathing gets rid of carbon dioxide waste and takes plenty of clean, fresh oxygen to your brain and muscles. More blood cells get the new, oxygen-rich air instead of the same old stale stuff. Experts estimate that proper breathing helps your body eliminate toxins 15 times faster than poor, shallow breathing. You'll not only be healthier, but you'll be able to perform better (mentally and physically) and, of course, be less stressed and more relaxed.

© Dan Smith

CHAPTER 11
Your 16-week Training Guide:
Weeks 9-12

You have 8 weeks of training under your belt and you should be noticing your improved fitness now. This next phase of training introduces more speedwork and intensity, which improves your ability to work hard. I have added some flippers into the swim workouts to help with leg strength and ankle flexibility. If your local pool doesn't have the equipment, look at investing in some.

11.1 WEEK 9

Total Training time: 4hr
All sessions RPE 1-2, with 3-4 indicated

Monday: OFF

Tuesday: Swim 35 minutes
100m warm-up, choice stroke
4 x 75m (15") kick with flippers (50m easy kick, 25m very hard kick, RPE 4)
8 x 25m (20") freestyle (as breath 5)
6 x 25m (20") freestyle with flippers (as blast first 15m RPE 4, easy to the end)
200m easy cool down, choice of stroke

Total: 1000m

Wednesday: Run/walk 30 minutes
5 minute warm-up run/walking
15 minute (as 30 seconds jog, 30 seconds faster than jog pace RPE 3, 30 seconds jog, 1 min recovery walk)
5 x (10 seconds strides, 50 seconds walk)
5 minute cool down walk
**Strides are short quick bursts of running that should feel fast. Focus on quick turnover, long stride length and good technique. Improved strength and flexibility for faster running.

Thursday: Bike 45 minutes (stationary)
15 minute warm-up spin
4 x (20 seconds left leg spinning, 40 seconds both, 20 seconds right, 40 seconds both)
2 minute recovery spin
5 x (45 seconds big gear – 50-60 cadence, 1:15 seconds recovery spin)
10 minute cool down spin
**Feel tension and power with big gear. If you do not have an odometer on your bike to show you your cadence, then, every few minutes, count how many times one leg rotates in 30 sec then multiply this by 2 to receive your cadence reading.

Friday: Swim 30 minutes
200m warm-up choice
8 x 25m (20") freestyle (DPS – keep counting strokes and try to achieve minimal stroke count possible!)
4 x 150m (30") as 100m freestyle easy/50m fast (RPE 4)
6 x 25m (20") freestyle (as 10m easy, blast to end RPE 4-5)
100m cool down, choice stroke

Total: 1250m
**If you watch the pace clock, you can start tracking your 50m splits and see your speed progress!*

Saturday: Run/walk 40 minutes
5 minute warm-up walking
2 x (4 minute jog, 1 minute walk)
4 x (15 seconds jog, 45 seconds faster than jog pace RPE 3)
2 minute jog
2 x (10 second stride with 50 seconds recovery walk)
10 minute cool down walk

Sunday: Bike 60 minutes
15 minute warm-up spin
3 x (45 seconds left leg, 15 seconds both, 45 seconds right leg, 1:15 both)
2 minute recovery spin
2 x (45 seconds standing RPE 4, 2:15 minute recovery spin)
3 x 3 minutes (with 1 minute recovery) of fast cycling (RPE 3) at 90-95 cd.
15 minutes cool down spin
**During the fast cycling, take note of your speed if you have a computer on your bike. Start at an effort that you can maintain for all 3 intervals; it is better to start conservatively.*

11.2 WEEK 10

Total Training time: 3hr 40min
All sessions RPE 1-2, with 3-4 indicated

This week will be quite similar to last week, continuing with the gradual progression of adding more speed, while maintaining your base. The speedwork and higher intensity training is harder on your body; make sure you stretch well, and continue to focus on good nutrition and recovery.

Monday: OFF

Tuesday: Swim 35 minutes
200m warm-up (as 50m freestyle, 50m backstroke, 50m kick, 50m freestyle)
6 x 50m (15") kick with flippers (25m easy kick, 25m very hard kick RPE4)
4 x 25m (10") freestyle drill (Breath 5)
6 x 25m (15") freestyle with flippers (as 2 at medium effort RPE 3, 1 hard effort RPE 4)
200m easy cool down, choice of stroke

Total: 1050m
**Breath 5: breathing every 5 strokes allows you to focus on rotation and pull, and excellent exhation underwater.

Wednesday: Run/walk 25 minutes
5 minute warm-up walking
10 minute (as 45 seconds jog, 15 seconds faster than jog pace RPE 3, 30 seconds jog, 1 minute walk)
5 x (15 seconds stride, 40 seconds jog, 1 minute walk)
5 minute cool down walk
**Strides are fast and controlled, strong and smooth.

Thursday: Bike 40 minutes (stationary)
10 minute warm-up spin
3 x (30 seconds left leg spinning, 15 seconds both, 30 seconds right, 45 seconds both)
2 minute recovery spin
3 x (30 seconds 90rpm, 30 seconds 100rpm, 30 seconds 110rpm, 30 seconds 120+ rpm, 2 minute recovery spin) *RPE will rise through the set as you spin harder.*
10 minute cool down spin
**If you do not have an odometer on your bike to show you your cadence, then, every few minutes, count how many times one leg rotates in 15 sec then multiply this by 4 to receive your cadence reading.

Friday: Swim 30 minutes

300m warm-up (as 100 Fr, 100 kk, 100 choice)

4 x 50m (20") freestyle DPS count *your strokes per 25m and try to achieve your lowest stroke yet!*

4 x 100m (25") freestyle (as 50m easy/50m medium effort RPE 3)

100m cool down, choice stroke

Total: 1000m

Saturday: Run/walk 40 minutes

5 minute warm-up walking

3 x (4 minute jog, 2 minute walk)

2 x (30 seconds jog, 15 seconds stride, 2:15 minute recovery walk)

10 minute cool down walk

Sunday: Bike 50 minutes

10 minute warm-up spin

4 x (30 seconds left leg, 15 seconds both, 30 seconds right leg, 1:15 seconds both)

3-minute recovery spin

4 x (20 seconds standing, 1:40 minute recovery spin)

4 x 3 minutes (with 1 minute recovery) of fast cycling (RPE 3) at 90-95 cd

15 minutes cool down spin

11.3 WEEK 11

Total Training time: 3hr 45min
All sessions RPE 1-2, with 3-4 indicated

This week will be quite similar to last week – we are gradually adding more speedwork into the progression, while maintaining your base.

Monday: OFF

Tuesday: Swim 25 minutes
200m warm-up (as 50m Fr, 50m bk, 50m kk, 50m fr)
8 x 25m (15") kicks freestyle with flippers (as 25m easy kick, 25m very hard kick)
6 x 50m (15") freestyle (25 freestyle at effort, 25 double arm backstroke)
200m easy cool down, choice of stroke

Total: 900m

Wednesday: Run/walk 30 minutes
5 minute warm-up walking
4 x (20 seconds stride, 40 seconds jog, 2 minute walk)
10 minutes (as 45 seconds jog, 15 seconds at effort – document HR after each, 2 minute walk)
5 minute cool down walk

Thursday: Bike 45 minutes (stationary)
10 minute warm-up spin
2 x (45 seconds left leg spinning, 15 seconds both, 45 seconds right, 45 seconds both)
2-minute recovery spin
3 x (30 seconds 90rpm, 30 seconds 100rpm, 30 seconds 110rpm, 30 seconds 120+ rpm –document HR , 2 minute recovery) *RPE will rise through the set as you spin harder.*
2 x (30 seconds at effort, 1:30 minute recovery)
10-minute cool down spin
**If you do not have an odometer on your bike to show you your cadence, then, every few minutes, count how many times one leg rotates in 15 sec then multiply this by 4 to receive your cadence reading.*

Friday: Swim 35 minutes
200m warm-up (as 100m fr, 50m kk, 50m choice)
4 x 75m (45") freestyle DPS
3 x 150m (45") (as 50m freestyle easy, 50m medium effort RPE 3, 50m backstroke)
100m cool down, choice stroke

Total: 1150m

Saturday: Run/walk 40 minutes
5 minute warm-up walking
3 x (45 seconds jog, 15 seconds stride, 2 minute recovery walk)
4 x (3 minute jog, 2 minute walk)
5 minute cool down walk

Sunday: Bike 50 minutes
15 minute warm-up spin
4 x (30 seconds left leg, 15 seconds both, 30 seconds right leg, 1:15 minute both)
3 minute recovery spin
3 x 4 minutes (with 2 minutes recovery) fast cycling with cadence 90-95, RPE 3
15 minutes cool down spin
**Doing the 4-minute faster riding intervals over the same course will allow you work hard to maintain speed.

11.4 WEEK 12

Total Training time: 3hr 55min
All sessions RPE 1-2, with 3-4 indicated

You are now almost at the 3 month mark of your training. This last week of this phase requires you to increase your effort once more, before a recovery week. If you have been doing your training over similar bike and run routes, you should notice that you cover more ground, or are going quicker than when we started.

Monday: OFF

Tuesday: Swim 25 minutes
200m warm-up (as 50m fr, 50m bk, 50m br, 50m fr)
4 x 25m (15") kick with flippers (25m easy kick, 25m very hard kick RPE 4)
8 x 25m (15") freestyle (alternate 25m freestyle fast RPE 4, 25m breaststroke or backstroke easy)
4 x 50m (25") freestyle with flippers (as 25m RPE 3, 25 at effort RPE 4)
200m easy cool down, choice of stroke

Total: 900m

Wednesday: Run/walk 30 minutes
5 minute warm-up walking
2 x (20 seconds stride, 40 seconds jog, 2 minute walk)
3 x (1 minute jog, 30 seconds fast PRE 4, 3 minute walk)
5 minute cool down walk

Thursday: Bike 45 minutes (stationary)
10 minute warm-up spin
1 x (30 seconds left leg spinning, 15 seconds both, 30 seconds right, 45 seconds both)
2 minute recovery spin
1 x (30 seconds 90rpm, 30 seconds 100rpm, 30 seconds 110rpm, 30 seconds 120+ rpm –document HR , 2 minute recovery spin)
4 x (1 minute at effort—document HR, 3 minutes recovery spin)
10 minute cool down spin
**If you do not have an odometer on your bike to show you your cadence, then, every few minutes, count how many times one leg rotates in 15 sec then multiply this by 4 to receive your cadence reading.

Friday: Swim 35 minutes
200m warm-up (as 50m fr, 100m kk, 50m choice)
2 x 75m (30") freestyle with fins (as 50m DPS, 25m at RPE 4)
5 x 100m (45") (as 50m freestyle easy/50m freestyle RPE 3)
100m cool down, choice stroke

Total: 1050m

Saturday: Run/walk 40 minutes
5 minute warm-up walking
2 x (45 seconds jog, 15 seconds stride, 2 minute recovery walk)
4 x (2 minute jog, 1 minute at RPE 4, 3 minute walk)
5 minute cool down walk

Sunday: Bike 50 minutes
15 minute warm-up spin
3 x (30 seconds left leg, 15 seconds both, 30 seconds right leg—document HR,
1:15 minute both
2 minute recovery spin
4 x 2 minutes fast riding (1 minute recovery) RPE 3-4, cd 90-95
15 minutes cool down spin

11.5   DID YOU KNOW?

While swimming freestyle, try to minimize your kick. Most people will kick extra hard to make up for lack of balance in the water. Minimizing your kick will allow you to improve your balance, as well as conserve energy.

© David McColm

CHAPTER 12
Your 16-week Training Guide: Weeks 13-16

You are now on the final stretch of your training plan. This Phase consists of an easy week to allow you to adapt to the last weeks of hard training. You then have two weeks of more intense training before leading into your goal race. In these last four weeks, you should start thinking ahead to race day and adding some transition practice onto the end of your sessions. This only has to be 10-15 minutes of drills to practice T1 and T2. See the section 'Transitions' in Chapter 4. Racing and transition is found in Chapter 5. Starting on week 13, your Sunday ride will start to incorporate Brick training, where you will be asked to walk or run right off the bike to get used to the feeling.

12.1 WEEK 13

Total Training time: 3hr 50min
All sessions RPE 1-2, with 3-4 indicated

Monday: OFF

Tuesday: Swim 30 minutes
100m warm-up choice
6 x 25m (10") kick (25m easy kick, 25m very hard kick RPE 4)
8 x 25m (15") freestyle (as 1 easy, 1 RPE 2, 1 at RPE 3, 1 at RPE 4)
3 x 150m (30") freestyle (as 50 easy, 50 RPE 4, 50 double arm backstroke)
200m easy cool down, choice of stroke

Total: 1200m

Wednesday: Run/walk 30 minutes
5 minute warm-up walking
1 x (15 seconds stride, 45 seconds jog, 1 minute walk)
4 x (2 minute jog, 30 seconds at RPE 3, 2 minute walk)
5 minute cool down walk

Thursday: Bike 50 minutes
10 minute warm-up spin
2 x (45 seconds left leg spin, 15 seconds both, 45 seconds right, 45 seconds both)
2 minute recovery spin
1 x (30 seconds 90rpm, 30 seconds 100rpm, 30 seconds 110rpm, 30 seconds 120+ rpm –document HR , 2 minute recovery spin)
3 x (2 minute at RPE 3, 1 minute at RPE 4, 3 minutes recovery)
10 minute cool down spin

Friday: Swim 20 minutes
200m warm up (as 50m fr, 100m kk, 50m choice)
6 x 25m (15") freestyle with fins (25m easy swim, 25m blast RPE 4-5)
3 x 100m (30") (as 50m freestyle DPS/50m backstroke)
100m cool down, choice stroke

Total: 750m

Saturday: Run/walk 50 minutes
8-10 minute warm-up walking
4 x (45 seconds jog at RPE 2, 15 seconds stride, 2 minute recovery walk)
4 x (2 minute run at RPE 1, 1 minute at RPE 2, 3 minute walk)
5 minute cool down walk

Sunday: Brick: Bike 50 minutes + walk 5 minutes right after the bike
10 minute warm-up spin
1 x (30 seconds left leg, 15 seconds both, 30 seconds right leg, 1:15 minute both)
Bike steady at RPE 2 until 50 minutes + walk 5 minutes right after bike.
**Brick: be ready to stop, get off your bike and start walking right away.

12.2 WEEK 14

Total Training time: 4hr 10min
All sessions RPE 1-2, with 3-4 indicated

Monday: OFF

Tuesday: Swim 35 minutes

200m warm-up (100m fr, 50m bk, 50m kk)
8 x 25m (10") freestyle (25m breath 5, 25m drill – fingertip drag)
4 x 50m (15") freestyle (1 easy, 1 at RPE 2, 1 at RPE 3, 1 at RPE 4)
4 x 100m (20") freestyle with flippers (as 50m easy, 50m concentrating on strong kick)
200m easy cool down, choice of stroke

Total: 1200m

Wednesday: Run/walk 35 minutes
5 minute warm-up walking
4 x (10 seconds stride, 50 seconds jog, 1 minute walk)
3 x (2 minute jog, 1 minute at RPE 4, 1 minute jog, 2 minute walk)
5 minute cool down walk

Thursday: Bike 40 minutes
10 minute warm-up spin
1 x (30 seconds left leg spinning, 15 seconds both, 30 seconds right, 45 seconds both)
3 minute recovery spin
4 x 2 minutes fast cycling RPE 3-4, cd 90+ (2 minutes recovery spin between efforts).
10 minute cool down spin
**During your fast cycling efforts, pay attention to your self talk: are you coaching yourself with positive talk and feedback?*

Friday: Swim 25 minutes
200m warm up (as 50m fr, 100m kk, 50m choice)
4 x 25m (20") freestyle (25m easy swim, 25m as 15m blast/10m easy,)
4 x 75m (30") (as 50m freestyle DPS/25m fast)
200m cool down, choice stroke

Total: 800m

Saturday: Run/walk 55 minutes
10 minute warm-up walking
4 x (10 seconds stride, 10 seconds jog, 1 minute walk)
4 x (2 minute medium fast run RPE 3, 2 minute recovery walk)
4 x (1 minute fast run RPE 4, 1 minute easy jog, 2 minute walk)
10 minute cool down walk

Sunday: Brick: Bike 60 minutes + jog 2 minutes/walk 3 minutes off bike
10 minute warm-up spin
3 x (45 seconds left leg, 15 seconds both, 45 seconds right leg, 1:15 minute both)
5 minute recovery spin
4 x 5 minutes fast cycling (with 3 minutes easy cycling recovery between) RPE 3, cd 90+
10 minutes cool down spin + jog easy 2 minutes/walk 3 minutes off bike
**Brick: be ready to stop, get off your bike and start jogging/walking right away.*

12.3 WEEK 15

Total Training time: 4hr 20min
All sessions RPE 1-2, with 3-4 indicated

This is your last week of hard training before you start to taper for your first race. You should feel confident that you have come this far. Do your best effort this week, stay positive and start getting excited about putting it all together in a triathlon soon. Re-read the sections on Getting Ready to Race to make sure you are prepared.

Monday: OFF

Tuesday: Swim 40 minutes
200m warm-up (100m fr, 50m bk, 50m kk)
8 x 50m (15") freestyle (as 25m breath 3, 25m breath 5)
8 x 25m (15") freestyle 2 x (1 easy, 1 at RPE 2, 1 at RPE 3, 1 at RPE 4)
4 x 100m (20") freestyle (as 50m glide to 3 drill, 50m at medium effort)
200m easy cool down, choice of stroke

Total: 1400m

Wednesday: Run/walk 35 minutes
5 minute warm-up walking
3 x (10 seconds stride, 50 seconds jog, 1 minute walk)
4 x (3 min faster running RPE 3, 1 minute walk)
5 minute cool down jog, 3 minute walk

Thursday: Bike 40 minutes
10 minute warm-up spin
2 x (20 seconds left leg spinning, 40 seconds both, 20 seconds right, 40 seconds both)
2 minute recovery spin
3 x 3 minutes fast riding RPE 3-4 with 3 minute easy recovery spin between
10 minute cool down spin

Friday: Swim 30 minutes
200m warm up (as 50m fr, 100m kk, 50m choice)
8 x 25m (15") freestyle (alternate 25m fast/25 DPS)
3 x 150m (45") freestyle (as 75m fingertip drag drill, 25m easy swim, 50m fast RPE 3)
200m cool down, choice stroke

Total: 1050m

Saturday: Run/walk 50 minutes
15 minute warm-up run/walking
5 x (10 seconds stride, 30 seconds jog, 1 minute walk)
3 x (3 minutes faster running RPE 3, 2 minute walk)
10 minute cool down jog, 5 minute walk

Sunday: Bike 65 minutes + run 10' off bike
15 minute warm-up spin
3 x (30 seconds left leg, 15 seconds both, 30 seconds right leg, 45 seconds both)
4 minute recovery spin
2 x 7 minutes faster riding RPE 3 with 3 minutes recovery riding between efforts
10 minutes cool down spin
Jog easy off bike 5 minutes, walk 5 minutes

12.4 WEEK 16

Total Training time: 2hr 45min
All sessions RPE 1-2, with 3-4 indicated

Congratulations! You have made it to the final week of the training plan. This is your taper week. You will rest and get fresh for your race this weekend. Instead of taking total rest, you will be training in light, but frequent doses to stay activated and fresh to race.

Monday: OFF

Tuesday: Swim 20 minutes
100m warm-up (50m fr, 50m kk)
2 x 50m (20") freestyle (25m breath 5, 25m breath 3)
2 x 25m (15") freestyle (1 easy, 1 blast)
5 x 100m (10") freestyle (as 50m fingertip drag drill, 50m medium effort)
100m easy cool down, choice of stroke

Total: 850m

Wednesday: Run/walk 15 minutes
5 minute warm-up jog/walk
3 x (10 seconds stride, 1:50 minute jog, 1 minute walk)
5 minute cool down walk/jog

Thursday: Bike 25 minutes
5 minute warm-up spin
2 x (2 minutes at RPE 3 with 3 minute recovery spin)
10 minute cool down spin

Friday: Swim 15 minutes
100m warm up (as 50m fr, 50m choice)
8 x 25 m freestyle (25m as 15m blast/10m easy, 25m easy, with 10 seconds rest)
200m freestyle straight easy swim
100m cool down, choice stroke

Total: 600m

Saturday: Run/walk 20 minutes OR REST
10 minute warm-up walking
4 x (30 seconds jog, 15 seconds stride, 1:45 minute walk)
5 minute easy jog
5 minute cool down walk

Sunday: RACE!

If you are still a couple of weeks out of your first race, assess how you feel and pick and choose some past workouts that will maintain your current fitness level, keep you motivated and rested at the same time!

12.5 DID YOU KNOW?

Along with physical gains, exercise offers many mental benefits. Regular exercise reduces stress by helping to dissipate the lactic acid that accumulates in your blood and sharpens your brain by increasing the amount of oxygen available. As well, it increases your production of endorphins - those little substances that create a sense of well-being and increase your body's resistance to pain, and stimulates the release of epinephrine, a hormone that creates a sense of happiness and excitement. So if you've had a hard day at work... the best thing to do is grab your runners and head out the door!

© Dan Smith

CHAPTER 13:
You Did It! Now What?

Congratulations on completing your first triathlon. Most importantly, Kudos to you for devoting yourself to the training required, for committing to a program and a goal and following through. Thanks to your own ability to organize your time and find a way, you have achieved your goal. You should feel proud. If you are like a lot of people who start triathlon, you were probably already setting new goals and looking for new events while you are were training for this one. In the back of your mind, you probably have a mental list of all the ways you want to improve and which races you think would be fun to try. You may already be dreaming about getting a new racing bike!

13.1 POST-RACE RECOVERY

The first thing you need to think of after completing a race, and especially if you have further goals, is recovery. Recovery does not mean putting your feet up and getting bed rest, as in 'recovery from the flu'. Recovery in sports is active, though easy, and actually refers to how well you can adapt to the hard work that you just put in.

Hard Work + Recovery = Adaptation = Better Performance.

Recovery refers to the state in which your body can adapt positively to the hard work you just did in order to make you stronger. Racing tends to stress your system more than training as athletes typically go harder (physical stress) and try harder (emotional stress) during key events. Failure to recover leads to poor adaptation to the stress which eventually may lead to injury, over-training and feelings of burn out.

How well you recover dictates when you can start training again but also how strong you will be when you re-start. Recovery should be built into your race plan: all too often athletes cross the finish line and think they are done for the day, when actually, recovery is a vital link to gaining benefit from what you just did.

Your post-race recovery starts within 15 minutes of the completion of your race. You should be getting some fluids back into your body and also eating about 200-300 calories (mainly carbohydrates, small amount of protein) for recovery. There is a short window of opportunity for optimal recovery. Athletes who neglect that short-term post race nutrition window often report higher degree of muscles soreness and tightness, due to the severe depleting of muscle energy and accumulation of lactic acid. Great post-race choices for replenishing glycogen in your muscles:

- White bread
- 250ml of chocolate milk, or milk
- A banana
- Melon
- Sports drink
- Cookies
- Raisins
- An energy bar or recovery bar like PowerBar sport

Another thing that you can do right away to aid recovery is to walk about to flush your legs, do a short spin on your bike and go back and swim in the lake gently. A gentle post race massage—if that is an option—can be great at flushing the legs as well.

Within several hours of the race, ensure you have a nutritious meal full of carbohydrates, lean protein and fresh vegetables. A glass of wine to celebrate is OK, but too much alcohol will impair your body's ability to work on repairing damage done at the cellular level. Alcohol and caffeine will also interfere with hydration and sleep, two other factors that are important to race recovery.

13.2 RACE RECOVERY CHECKLIST

After the Race

- Eat/drink recovery food within 15 minutes
- Walk about or move
- Stretch a little

That Night

- Eat a nutritious meal
- Get a massage or do self massage
- Stretch
- Sleep

Planning recovery in the days after a race is important for several reasons. Firstly it gives you distinct parameters for your sessions following a race, allowing your body to repair and strengthen after the extreme effort, even when you are mentally ready to train hard. Just as in training, recovery from races allows you to come back a stronger athlete and make consistent improvements. Secondly, when planning your racing season, taking recovery into consideration will allow you to choose races that take you to a peak and don't dig you further and further into a hole. Racing every weekend might seem like fun at first, but that lack of emotional and physical recovery will likely shorten your season.

Keeping a journal after races and hard sessions will allow you to, over time, figure out what sort of an athlete you are and what it takes to recover from various distances.

The duration and importance of recovery depends on several factors, not the least of which is individual recovery time. Some of us still can't run down a hill three weeks following an Ironman, others are skipping about several days later. How much you tapered into an event and how important the event is also play a role. You taper longer and 'give' more in your regional championships mid-season than you did running the Santa Clause fun run at Christmas, and need longer recovery.

A sprint or an Olympic distance usually requires 4-7 days recovery and this depends on the athlete and how sore they are after the event. Often an athlete will feel fantastic the day right after a great performance, and will 'fly' during a run session, as they are still on a high from the positive emotional event. The second day is often the worst day for tiredness, called the 'delayed onset of fatigue'. The third day an athlete can do some light aerobic work and then by the fourth day can usually get in a longer session. As with most things, listening to your body is the best thing you can do.

A recovery period is also a mental refresher, as the days leading up to an event can be stressful and full of intense emotions and emotional control. It is also a good time to review the race, taking notes about what went well, what didn't go so well and what you would do differently the next time you race and are faced with the same situation.

Use your recovery period as a chance to take a break, but still enjoy your activities without any pressure to perform. Schedule massage in your recovery period and fill some of the spare time you have with stretching sessions. Concentrate on good nutrition and hydration; these are favors you do to a body that is trying hard to repair.

13.3 LEARNING FROM YOUR RACE: DEBRIEFING

Successful athletes review their races, taking an honest look at what went on, what they did well and what they could have done better. It is generally advisable to let several days pass before you do a debriefing. This is for several reasons: if your race went especially well, your 'emotional high' and feelings of being superhuman might prevent you from looking at areas you could improve. Likewise, if the race was disappointing, it will be hard for you to reflect clearly at first. A few days usually clear the air and we can move on and get back to work.

After several days reflection it helps to talk over your race with a coach or some other person you trust. Writing down your thoughts is also a good idea.

Make some notes about things that you did well before, and in the race. Perhaps the run didn't go as planned, but don't overlook the way that you prepared for the race, or the way you executed the swim and bike. One failed component of a race is just that. Triathlons, by their three sport nature, present us with many ways to both excel and fail! Don't look at the post race debrief as an analysis of your worthiness, but as a chance to give yourself some new goals and to appreciate what you just did.

Be aware of factors that were entirely out of your control, like weather, draft marshals and other competitors' actions and keep that in perspective. This is a case of having to be entirely philosophical about the circumstances for the failure. Regroup and move on from these types of disappointments.

Lucy reflects: Disappointment

There are 3 general sport philosophies that I have developed over the years as an athlete and a coach:

1. Try to avoid making big decisions or career changes when things aren't going well or after a subpar performance.

It's easy to react emotionally or irrationally after a disappointment. It's better to make the big decisions after a good race, or after taking a reasonable amount of time to sit back and reflect and think with a clear mind. Several times after a big event that goes wrong athletes have said to me, „that's it, I'm doing something different" or „I don't want to do this anymore". After a few weeks they realize that maybe some adjustments do

need to be made, but not a career overhaul or monumental changes.

2. Never punish yourself for a subpar performance in a race or practice. Look at what could have done better, but don't beat up on yourself for what you didn't do right.

There is always something positive you can take out of a race or a practice. In Ironman Canada we had a pro triathlete fit and tapered for her first Ironman. She had worked hard for the race and had done an excellent job in training. Before she could even get on the bike, she got tangled up in another competitor's race wheel in T1 and cut her foot open, and her day was over. She was extremely disappointed at not being able to compete over her two

13.4 POST-RACE CHECKLIST FOR LEARNING

- How was my week before taper and mental state?
- How did registration go; what would I do differently?
- How was my race morning prep and nutrition?
- How was my emotional state on race morning?
- How did transition set up go? Did I have everything I needed?
- How was my warm-up? Would I do the same again?
- How was the start?
- Evaluate the swim, bike and run from a technical perspective and by how focused you were.
- Evaluate your transitions. Were they smooth, calm, fast?
- How did you deal with late race fatigue?
- How did you deal with your competition?
- How was your immediate and delayed recovery?

favorite and strongest disciplines, and down on herself for not avoiding the transition zone mishap. We reflected and decided that the process of the training will still make her stronger for the next one, and the mental prep involved with getting ready for a major competition and dealing with the nerves, etc, is an important skill to develop, and she had done a good job at this. We also decided that she needed to gain a better understanding of transition work before the race, and to try and anticipate any tricky areas.

3. Every workout or race is NOT the World Championships—you don't have to prove yourself every time you go out. Know what the purpose of the workout or race is and complete it appropriately. Go easy when you should go easy and *go hard when it's time to hammer. Have goals for your sessions and not always just time or outcome oriented goals, but also technique, focus and enjoyment. Make adjustments if the goals aren't being met. Decide that your confidence is not going to be determined by the result of one or a few workouts. Recognize that everyone has his or her good and bad days, and consistency (physical and mental) is more important. You can't „shoot the lights out" every session.*

From this checklist, you will be able to pull out some key learning and also find areas that you would like to improve. It might also bring up questions that when answered by another more experienced triathlete or coach, will further buoy your experience and knowledge of the sport.

If you continue to focus on what you want to learn and accomplish, it will be easier to plan your next race and short-term goals, and to start thinking ahead to how you want to execute an even greater performance.

You will be able to identify some new goals but at the very least, it will give you a snapshot of your first race and will specifically capture exactly what you accomplished. This should make you feel great about yourself and further embed you in this terrific sport!

13.5   MOVING ON AND UP: NEW GOALS

Now that you have gone through the experience of training for an event and have one triathlon under your belt, you have a much better idea of the sport and what it takes. This newfound knowledge is a great platform from which to set new goals for yourself and create further life opportunities that you are proud of and which are very rewarding. You will have gained a good idea of your skills over the three sports, the time it takes to train and, if you are honest with yourself, just how competitive you want to be.

As you have probably realized, having clear priorities goes a long way in what approach you will take towards your next race. After you have made that list of areas where you can improve, you can begin to set goals. Before defining the goals for yourself, some important questions need to be asked.

- How committed am I to improving this aspect of my triathlon? Athletes have to take ownership of goals for them to become reality.

- Do these goals actually fit within my life priorities? If you want to shave 15 minutes off your 3.8k swim, will you want to or be able to go to the pool 2-3 more times each week?

SETTING NEW GOALS

Using the „list for possible improvements" that you have devised from your season analysis, plus the knowledge of your commitment and priorities, you can now start to write down your future goals. Things to keep in mind when writing your goals:

- Start with process versus outcome goals. Process goals are based mainly on tasks that you have as much control over a possible, such as training schedules, sport skills and racing relaxed.
- Make your goals realistic, measurable and achievable. Improving times for a set distance, improving bike handling skills and getting a handle on pre-race stress are all measurable goals that you will be able to analyze after the fact. Being 'happy' is hard to measure, so try to be specific.

ACHIEVING YOUR GOALS

Your goals are written down, and you really feel committed to achieving them next season and becoming a better triathlete. Now you need to assess what you have to do in order to get there or else it's just words on paper. This is where the road map comes in. On the way to the big goals, you take a path, and set smaller milestones. As you reach these smaller milestones you will be able to assess whether you are still on the right track to reaching your goals and can have small triumphs along the way that keep you motivated. At this point you might start using outside resources.

- Do you have the skills necessary to improve your swimming, biking to running on your own?
- Do you need a coach, should you attend a triathlon camp, join a local club or get some reference books?
- Support (financially and from friends and significant others), travel, equipment are other resources to consider.

Most likely you have been thinking about your next race before you even were halfway through this one. This sport is infectious and there are so many opportunities to create personal success and fun. The commitment to progressing and improving season after season is all part of the game.

Every footstep counts. Every time you race or train you have the opportunity to achieve. Whether it is something extraordinary is largely up to you and your attitude.

CHAPTER 14
Final Thoughts

As with any technical subject, the scope of information that could be included in this book is massive. I have attempted to add as much of the essential beginner's information that I can, with my discretion being based upon my long history of helping beginners in triathlon and running and of coaching athletes to their goals. At one point in my career I was also a beginner triathlete and had so many questions that were answered by friends, coaches and by just going to races. I didn't have the Internet or Google when I started in triathlon, and had to rely mostly on asking questions. My goal for this book was to percolate all those questions into one manual that is both useful and practical while also capturing what is exciting about this sport.

I have tried to frame the 'How To's' using my own wisdom, which has been a weaving together of the intricacies of racing and training with what I have learned from twenty years of high performance racing and fifteen years of coaching. Some of the information might be more than you need right now, but I hope you will be able to revisit my tips on training, goal setting, race preparation and racing over and over as you learn and improve.

Having a great coach can really improve your opportunities for success. Triathlon can be all encompassing so having an expert build your training program and support you with great advice generally leads to great success. If you have found the advice in this book valuable you may want to contact LifeSport for coaching. More information is available at: www.lifesportcoaching.com

LifeSport Coaching is a proud to be the "Official Coaches of Ironman". LifeSport and Ironman have joined together to provide world-class coaching, training programs, and training camps for athletes competing in Ironman, 70.3 or shorter distance triathlons. LifeSport believes that excellent coaching should be available to anyone who has the desire to achieve their personal goals. Led by Olympic Gold Medal, 70.3 and Ironman coaches Lance Watson and Paul Regensburg, LifeSport offers personalized, systematic, and interactive training to athletes of all abilities.

At LifeSport our philosophy is based on providing customized training progressions while the athlete gains an education in both the sport and themselves. LifeSport training is structured to meet the athlete's goals by building a program that compliments the athlete's individual needs and lifestyle. With LifeSport coaches, there are no wasted workouts and no junk miles. LifeSport is proud to have coached numerous age group athletes to amazing accomplishments like completing their very first event, achieving personal records, and qualifying for Ironman World Championship Events. Our coaching interaction and personalized coaching programs emphasize fitness, performance and inspiration for all of our clients. The custom designed programs are guaranteed to help you achieve your goals and dreams.

Contact us and see how we can build the perfect program for you!

© Bakke-Svensson/Ironman

Acknowledgements

I would like to acknowledge LifeSport Coaching for giving me the opportunity to write this book for beginners. LifeSport founders Lance Watson and Paul Regensburg have been integral to my development as a coach and an athlete.

© Frank Lucarelli

They are both immensely helpful with knowledge, ideas and resources whenever I need a question answered. Being married to one of the best triathlon coaches in the world has made a huge impact on my own development as an athlete and a coach, and I have been blessed to have such a mentor. Further, I have been able to use a lot of coaching information and documents that we have on hand at LifeSport and for that I am grateful.

For his valuable input and comments with photos, I would like to thank LifeSport coach Dan Smith. For their enthusiasm for the triathlon lifestyle, I would like to thank the rest of the LifeSport coaches for being a part of an awesome team: Mark Overton, Mark Shorter, Christopher Thomas, D'arcey Musselman, Jessica Depew and Bjoern Ossenbrink.

Thanks to Brian Baker and Frank Lucarelli at PowerBar Canada for immense nutritional support and information over the years in helping make race day a success for me and the athletes I coach.

Thank you to my sister Jo Smith, who has written so many of her own chapters for her PhD in biology that she was a huge support around 'getting the job done'.

And thank you to my husband Lance, who willingly took on extra 'Dad' duty with Maia and Ross on quite a few mornings, so that I could get up at 5:30 a.m. and write this book. Our life is a triathlon of sport, kids and love.

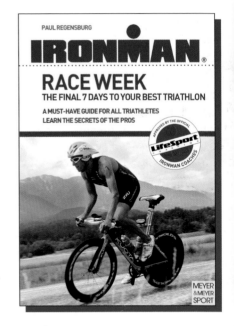

PHOTO CREDITS

Cover photo: © fotolia/jon11

Photos: see individual photos

Cover design: Sabine Groten